PHONE MONKEY

ANONYMOUS

phonemonkeybooks

BOOK ONE:
TRAINING

Introduction

Clive sat opposite me in the call centre where we sold home, motor and a few other insurance-type things. As a look of panic spread across his weary face, I thought I'd best prick up my ears and listen to what was happening. He had a customer on the line who he would never forget.

Clive: Hi there, how can I help today?

Customer: Well, I thought I'd best ring you about my insurance. I'm eighty-two years old, you see.

Clive: Okay... and what can I do for you?

Customer: Well, I didn't know if I had to inform you or not, but my doctor sent me up to the hospital for an eye test, and I've just been registered blind.

Clive: So are you wanting to cancel your car insurance?

Customer: Oh no, sonny. I just thought I had to tell you if I had any medical conditions in case it affected my insurance.

Clive: So you're blind, and still driving your car?

Customer: Yes, but it's not a problem.

Clive: This might sound like a silly question, but why is it not a problem that you're driving when you can't see?

Customer: Well I've always got Harold with me.

Clive: Is that your husband?

Customer: No, my guide dog.

Clive (stunned for a second): So let me get this straight, you're still driving the car even though you're blind, but it's okay because you have your guide dog Harold in the car with you?

Customer: That's right. He sits in the front seat and barks out instructions to help me with my driving.

Clive: It sounds awfully dangerous to me, I'm not sure if we can provide motor insurance for blind people. Let me just check through some other details on your policy first and we'll go from there. So it says here that you've held your licence for thirty-seven years, is that right?

Customer: What, a driving licence?

Clive: Yeah.

Customer: Oh no, I don't have my own, I use my husband's.

Clive: You don't have your own driving licence?

Customer: No, I'm a good driver, I've never needed to take my test. My husband said I was really good behind the wheel and that I was okay to share his licence.

Clive: So you're blind and your guide dog directs you through traffic, and you've never had a driving licence?

Customer: That's right.

Clive: Oh dear.

Welcome to the world of the Phone Monkey; a poor group of individuals who toil away in call centres across the world for very little money, usually to pay off their student debt or to earn just enough to be able to move out of their parents' house.

After three years of going through the poverty of self-employment, I decided to dive headfirst into the world of the call centre, and this book covers my first 18 months of this long, but never boring, journey.

Day One

I'd decided to err on the side of caution and make sure I was on a bus which gave me plenty of time to get to work, which I suppose in a way it did. I was there over an hour early, and the building wasn't even open. But still, at least it wasn't the middle of winter and I wasn't stood around shivering my nads off. Oh wait, yes I was.

Thankfully the receptionist turned up a few minutes later and I finally got inside, and was told where the coffee machine was… but that's not the extent of it. It was free. All the hot drinks were free! I know to most of you this will sound like something completely normal for an office environment, but to me this was new. And VERY exciting. I was very easily pleased. So over the next forty or so minutes I trundled backwards and forwards to the coffee machine, trying a variety of different hot drinks (white tea, black tea, lattes, decaffeinated cappuccinos, a selection of soups), before the rest of my fellow Phone Monkeys arrived.

Four of us had met before, at a welcome evening which we came to the previous week, where we had discussed our hours and what the job was going to entail. The most interesting and enlightening aspect of this welcome evening was that we got to sit with actual Phone Monkeys while they did their job, and listen in to their calls. My personal Phone Monkey was Shahid, who explained the bonus scheme to me. "Basically, we can offer up to a 40% discount on most of our insurance policies, but we offer as little as possible, let's say 5%. For each percentage point that you don't give to the customer, you get one point on your bonus, with each point equaling roughly 5p. So if they want to renew their insurance with us then great, we know we're getting this bonus, but if they definitely want to cancel, don't bother trying to persuade them otherwise, just cancel it and move on to the next customer as soon as possible. Be polite but brief with them and get onto your next call, 'cause we're all only here for the money, it's not a labour of love, and the next call could have a bonus attached to it."

This opened my eyes to this strange new world. First of all, I had no idea that bonuses could be such a large amount of money; I was happy with the salary on its own, without a bonus attached to it. I worked out that I could probably earn around £100 per week just in bonuses, and suddenly my initial reservations about joining the ranks of the Phone Monkey were put to one side, in favour of me one day becoming a millionaire. I had clearly entered a whole new plane of existence where your merits as a seller would actually be reflected in your pay. More importantly, we were in Retentions, but none of the Phone Monkeys had any intention of putting any real effort into retaining their fleeing customers as there would always be another customer, with a potentially higher bonus, on the next call.

After doing the usual meet-and-greet with my five fellow New Monkeys, we were informed that our trainer was running half an hour late. Two months ago, when I passed my job interview and they sent out all the information packs, I distinctly remember there been something in there about how punctuality was their main focus, because if we were late, calls wouldn't be answered and the business would lose money. Half an hour turned into an hour but eventually our teacher/trainer/life guru, Leanne, sauntered over and with no hint of an apology for her tardiness, threw us all into a room and began what would become the long and arduous process of training us Regular Human Beings into Phone Monkeys.

The first day was actually not too bad after that. It was a dedicated HR-day, which basically meant we sat chatting to each other from 10am to 5pm, interrupted only by coffee and meal breaks, of which there were many. Apparently this was 'Team-Building Time', but I didn't understand the merits of knowing how many tattoos Laura had on her bum, or whether Jack preferred Burger King to McDonalds. I wondered if we'd be tested on this trivia in the final exam?

Roadworks began right outside work that afternoon, meaning that the bus (which would usually take 5-10 minutes from work to town) actually took an hour. So I was stuck there listening to some weird goth playing System Of A Down WAY too loud in her headphones, watching a sophisticated-looking gent pick his nose and wipe it on his seat, and wondering to myself, has that sweet old lady with her eyes closed been on this bus so long that she's died?

Still, this was just day one. It surely couldn't get any worse than this over the next five weeks of training, could it?

Data Protection

Day Two

After checking out the bus timetables the night before, I managed to arrive at work at a reasonable hour today. I was still forty-five minutes early and I was the only member of staff in the building though. Not to worry, there were all those free hot drinks to devour.

I think it would be prudent of me to introduce you to the people in my training group here, if only so you can develop a love or hatred for them as this story progresses. There were six of us in total, four males and two females.

I'll start with myself here, not because I'm narcissistic about these things (although I am writing an autobiography, so who knows?), but because I feel that knowing a bit about me will help ease you into this story. I'd just hit my thirtieth year on this planet, and over the last fourteen years I'd had a number of jobs, all in different fields, none of which had gone anywhere. I'd been a library assistant, a cinema usher, an accountant, a trainee advertising artist, a file clerk, an industrial cleaner, and I'd run my own business selling books and toys online. The decision to start selling insurance was not an easy one for me to make, for one simple reason: I hate work. I am officially the laziest person in the world. The only reason I was self-employed for so long was because it meant I could get up in the morning, do an hour's work, then spend the rest of the day watching films, drinking wine and hanging out with my unemployed friends.

Now I was officially in my thirties, that all had to stop. I had to discover what it was like to be a responsible adult. I'd avoided it for twenty-nine years but suddenly work was there to bite me on the bum. Suddenly I was thinking about settling down and buying a house, and apparently you can't save for a house when you only earn about seven grand a year. So I sat down one day at the laptop and applied for about twenty jobs, and as luck would have it, I had a phone call from this insurance company the very next day, who invited me for an interview. It was pretty straightforward and suddenly I had my first Phone Monkey job! I think that's all you need to know about me for now. I'll try and fill you in on more details of my professional life as this story progresses. Now I'd like you to meet the rest of my training group...

Simon

For the sake of this story we're going to refer to him as Gay Simon. It's nothing to do with homophobia on mine or anyone else's part, I promise, it's just that it was impossible to have a conversation with him without him pointing out that he was gay at some point. He'd apparently had every job under the sun... He'd been a manager at McDonalds, he'd worked on the docks (I didn't probe any deeper into that one as there's no docks anywhere near where we live, and I was a little concerned it might be some kind of sexual metaphor), and he was so excited about becoming a Phone Monkey. There's something you need to know about Gay Simon though: Every single word that came out of his mouth was a complete fabrication. As we progress I'll fill you in on some of the unbelievable things he said.

Claire

I mean this in as polite a way as this term can be used... Claire was the MILF of the group. She was in her early forties but easily looked ten years younger. She'd lived in New York since she was 18, rent-free, in the house of some man she and her friend bumped into on the street (but she swears she never slept with him). She'd recently moved back to England and got married to a man she adored, and about whom she talked all the time. She had two kids who, like her, were obsessed with designer clothes, shoes and handbags. She was a lovely woman with no malice in her whatsoever, who would go out of her way to do anything for anyone.

Clive

"Young Clive", as I called him, was an intellectual student-type who, I'll be honest, seemed far too educated to be answering a phone for a living. He had a law degree and was planning to go back to university to do his Master's in Law at the end of the year. He would always buy a muffin before work, and insisted on reading the intellectual newspapers, unlike myself, who read the free newspaper that they handed out on the bus every day.

Laura

That is the last time you're going to hear her referred to by that name in this book. From here on in, she will be known only as Photo-Memory Girl. She was officially the most stupid person I've ever met. Looking at her Facebook profile was like trying to read Arabic. She wrote in that new-fangled text-speak that all the kids use these days, but somehow managed to get it so utterly wrong that her every post came across as gibberish. She thought she was absolutely beautiful. She was not. As soon as we started learning our first few bits of information about home insurance, she announced to everyone that she was finding the work really easy because she had a photographic memory. As it turned out, she really was as thick as she seemed and she did not have a photographic memory at all. She spent a lot of time with Gay Simon, and in fact those two kind of alienated themselves from the rest of us as they were the only smokers in the group. Those two disappearing at every given opportunity only gave us time to gossip freely about them. She was 21 years old, and the first time I met her I thought she was about 35. She applied her make-up at least twenty times a day, with a trowel. She had a good face for radio, as they say.

Jack

Similar to Clive, James was also massively over-educated to be working in a call centre. He was very talkative, constantly interrupting people, but not in an annoying way. In fact he was the first among us to pull Gay Simon up on his out-there stories, and a bit of hatred was developing between the two of them for just this reason. Jack had quite a short fuse and wasn't afraid to speak his mind. I think he knew that if he were to be sacked from this job, he could easily walk into any similarly-paying job with no trouble at all. He always wore a jumper to work, and they were always too small for him. Where I sat on the opposite side of the room, I could always see a bit of his belly poking out from under his jumper.

Part of our training today was drawing big posters of things you could insure. After we'd coloured in our pretty posters, we had a nice nap and a bit of a cuddle.

Photographic Memory Girl

Day Three

By this point, I'd decided I didn't like working nine to five. I didn't like working at all to be honest, but having to get to work early, and spend all day doing the same thing just had no appeal for me. If I wanted to have a day of doing nothing but watching bad TV and eating snacks, I would have to actually book that time off in advance now! How was I supposed to know which days I wasn't going to feel like doing any work? I didn't know how people could do this year after year. I suppose this is making me sound like a bit of a lazy whinger, but I genuinely believed I wasn't built for this kind of thing. On top of the work issue, when I got home I would now have to spend the next two hours writing up my experiences for my blog (which eventually became this book) for the next five weeks that I was in training. I hope you appreciate all the hard work I've put in for you, dear reader. And little did I know, my blog was going to extend way past the initial training period.

I expected another easy day of cuddles and naps, but sadly they wanted us to do some real work. Every day we were given two or three booklets full of information which we had to digest in preparation for a test which we would sit at the end of each week. We also got given little tasks to do. Yesterday's was doing big posters of various things, including the 10 Major Risks for which you're covered on your home insurance (things like fire, theft, flood etc). After being asked to create our own insurance companies and explain why we'd done certain things with our new fake companies, we were then told that everything we'd written was wrong. How productive. Why didn't they just teach us to do it right instead of trying to make us feel like buffoons? They were, after all, Phone Monkeys just like us a few years ago and must feel our pain about being on the bottom rung of the ladder!

*　　*　　*　　*　　*

At this point, I'd like to introduce a couple of new themes to the book. As I said earlier, I've had a lot of jobs, and a lot of strange things have happened to me over the course of my "career", and also during my time at university. As we go along I'd like to share some of these stories with you, for you to be able to build up a better idea in your head of the kind of person I am and how I ended up where I am now. I'm not entirely sure this will be in my best interests because you might find me to be an intolerable idiot, but hey, I can only try. At times the stories might seem completely unrelated to what I'm talking about in my current job, but please bear with me; there's a bigger picture.

Eleven years ago I was at university. I'd done an Art Diploma and then had three months off for the summer, before I was due to start my degree in Animation in the September. During these three months I was able to claim unemployment benefits, but they kept insisting on sending me to job interviews for things I had absolutely no interest in. One that sticks in my mind was for the job of Potato Peeler and Pot Washer in the kitchen of a big hotel. I knew full well that I didn't want a job, and by this point I was only a month away from starting my full-time degree so even if I got a job it would be very short-lived. I dressed as scruffily as I could, didn't even bother having a shower or a shave, then went to meet the head chef of this kitchen. I remember sitting at the table, and every time he asked me a question I'd mumble my reply, trying my absolute hardest not to get this job. He asked me if I was any good at peeling potatoes, so I told him I didn't know; I'd never tried before. Anyone who knows me now will know that that's simply not true. I love cooking, and even if I didn't, peeling a potato isn't exactly difficult. I knew I had to come across as some kind of inbred idiot.

Then he asked me how quickly I could wash pots. Thinking on my feet, I told him that my girlfriend did all our pots so I didn't have a clue how long it would take, but I wouldn't be able to have the water too hot as that might bring me out in a rash and make my hands swell up. My genius plan worked: I didn't get the job, and instead I had a long hot summer of drinking cider in the garden.

*   *   *   *   *

That's another theme which may come up again throughout the course of this book: Alcohol has not been my friend. Some might say that this is why it took me fourteen years to get my first "proper" job, but I'll let you decide for yourself.

Please Accept Our Condolences

Day Four

Photo Memory Girl and Gay Simon had spent the last three days claiming they were going to be the best salespeople on their teams, and how they were "born to do this job". They were so eager to get to the part where they spoke to actual customers, but today made our trainer, Leanne, see them for what they really were: A couple of idiots.

We'd all been making good progress on the packs of information we'd been asked to absorb, so Leanne decided we were ready to sit our first test a day early. The four of us who were… let's say 'normal'… were a little apprehensive about doing a test, but good ol' Gay Simon and Photo-Memory Girl were so confident about what they'd learnt with their "fantastic ability to absorb information" that we headed for the assessment room and did the test.

Gay Simon and Photo-Memory Girl failed it.

Jack, Claire, Clive and I all had a good old snigger behind their backs. I got 100% in the test but I'm not one to brag about such things. Despite this, Gay Simon decided that from that point on he was going to call me Brain Box.

When I was at school I probably had a similar nickname. I was good at art from an early age, and I wasn't shy in telling people about it. I would always brag that I couldn't wait for the next art lesson so I could hand in my homework and get yet another A*. I really was an insufferable little oik (I would describe myself in harsher terms but given that this is an all-ages book, it's probably best that I don't). My bragging finally came to an end when I was about 14, when our drama lesson was cancelled one day and converted into a session of everyone explaining to the teacher why my boasting about my abilities was making them depressed. I kid you not. After that I decided it was probably best to keep my thoughts about my skills to myself, and I'm definitely much more grounded these days.

Given that my artistic talents eventually amounted to nothing, I'm sure any of my old school friends would now be fully justified in approaching me and gloating about how little I'd achieved with these talents I used to enjoy talking endlessly about. Although I guess now that this book is published I can finally claim to be a published artist, I suppose, for drawing monkeys.

For the rest of the day, Gay Simon and Photo-Memory Girl had to go over all the course material again, using their supposed superior intellect to absorb the information we'd been given. This gave the other four us the chance to sit and talk all afternoon, about our lives.

*   *   *   *   *

Towards the end of my degree in animation, I realised that I was probably not going to be able to find any work in that field after graduation, so I started looking for other options. A friend of mine, George, was working in a care home, looking after kids who'd been abandoned by their parents, or mistreated and removed from their parents' custody. They were basically just looking after these kids until they could find new homes for them, but a lot of them went out to foster homes, suffered more abuse, and returned to this care home. Some of the stories George told me were heartbreaking, so I not only started considering going into the same field of work as a viable option, I also decided to interview him at length about his experiences, and make a short film about the job for the final major project of my degree.

I did a fair bit of research on care homes in general, and about the kinds of scenarios that put the children in these places, and prepared a long list of questions to ask George. The interviews ran for around two hours, all fully recorded, as I intended to use George's voice on my video, although heavily distorting it so as to not reveal his identity. What went on in the care homes was a matter of data protection and I didn't want to get him into trouble. He never gave me the kids' real names anyway, so there was no specific breach of confidentiality, but I thought it'd be safer not to risk it.

I spent the next two months writing out a script based on the interviews, so as to form some sort of coherent plot, following one child in particular, an eight-year-old called Danny (not his real name), who was a... how do I put this politely? A smearer. The years of suffering he'd received from his parents, and then from supposedly trustworthy foster parents, had messed with his head and he was uncontrollable.

Anyway, with the script finished, storyboards all drawn out, and half the soundtrack recorded (a mixture of the interviews and my own music), I took all my work into university to present it to my lecturers and see if they had any advice or help they could offer when I came to filming scenes for the short movie. I wasn't prepared for their response.

I was told that the subject matter was too close to the bone, and that they didn't want the university to be associated with the project in any way. I told them I would be handling it in a sensitive manner; I'd done a lot of research and had a fairly good idea of what I was talking about, and the short film might even bring the university some praise for probing into a subject matter which is generally brushed under the carpet as if these atrocities didn't happen. I was shot down. They refused point blank to look at my storyboards, read my script, or even consider the project. They said that even if I made the film they would refuse to watch it, would not mark it, and would therefore not be able to give me a degree off the back of it. I'd spent the first three months of my final year at university producing hundreds of pages of work for something which would now ultimately never see the light of day.

Devastated by my tutors' lack of faith in me, or lack of belief in the subject matter, I decided to avoid university for the next few months. I stopped attending lectures, didn't go to any of the presentations I was supposed to be giving to my tutors about my work in progress, and just generally developed a loathing for all things academic.

Then I had an idea: If they want a short film, but not one about care homes, I'd make them one. At this point I was living in a massive old house that, ironically, used to be a care home, and it had huge sprawling gardens which at night were extremely dark, lit only by dim orange floodlights. I got one of my friends to bring his video camera down one night and after a drink or two I said, "Right, follow me. Let's make this film."

I then proceeded to be filmed walking around the gardens and basement of this spooky old house. Naked.

I've always been a bit of a naturist, so to my friends, this was not something new, but I was sure that when my university lecturers saw it, they'd be shocked, to say the least. The theme of the film was basically that the main character was a frustrated songwriter who couldn't find fame, and decided to kill himself. One section of the video showed a close-up of my wrist as I stuck a craft knife into it, and dug deep as I dragged the knife up my arm. This was all camera trickery. I'd press on a little bit with the knife, stop filming, add fake blood, move the knife a little more, add more fake blood, and so on, until it appeared that I'd gouged a six-inch wound into my arm once it was all edited together. I was impressed with how realistic it all looked. I had a few drinks after I'd filmed that scene, then went to bed.

The following morning, I woke to find blood all over my bedsheets (this was a recurring pattern with me, you'll discover later). When I'd been pretending to cut my wrists I'd pressed on slightly too hard, and actually cut through my arm. Because of all the fake blood I'd used, I never realised at the time. I'd made this short film in the last few days before the end of my degree, so I could just present them with the film and wave goodbye before they could tell me it wasn't exactly what they were looking for. So I handed the video to the woman in charge of the showreel for the presentation evening, gave all my sketchbooks to my tutors, and went on my merry way.

What I hadn't realised at this point was that all the films we'd made were going to be shown on a cinema-size screen in a lecture theatre, on the presentation evening. Parents, brothers, sisters, tutors, and many others flocked through the doors to see what their wonderful family and friends had been creating, and spending three years of their life doing. When they showed my film there were gasps of horror, as I appeared fully naked in my film, and then slowly, gorily, killed myself. To make matters worse, as I'd only made the film a few days earlier, my arms were still bandaged up from the actual, albeit less serious, wounds I'd inflicted on myself during the filming of it. People kept asking me if I was okay, and if I was seeking therapy, but to me it was all a big joke.

The only other time I went into university after that was to collect my final grade. My tutors wouldn't talk to me. I'd always found them rude and unapproachable but now, after the whole nudity/suicide thing, it had become unbearable. I took my envelope and disappeared, smiling slyly to myself as I saw that the external examiners had given me a 2:1. Mission accomplished.

The Cupboard Of Doom

Day Five

After about five minutes of learning about putting Accidental Damage cover on people's home insurance, I had to run out of the room so I could puke a bit in the toilets. Nothing to do with the subject we were learning; I just seemed to constantly have a cold. Since my housemate's daughter started school a year ago, she'd been bringing a new cold home every week, which she'd passed on to me and everyone around me, who then all passed it back to me a second time. A sore throat wasn't much use to you when you sang in a band like I did, either. It was kind of embarrassing having to run out of the training room every five minutes. I had a suspicion that our trainer may have thought I was incontinent.

I'd tell you more about my day but I felt truly horrific, so my memories of those events are a little blurry.

Day Six

Monday mornings were always good for finding out the embarrassing things people had said and done over the weekend, and today was no exception. Photo-Memory Girl had gone out with Gay Simon on Friday night, to have a bit of a drinking session with him and his boyfriend and along the way, about five pints in, she was introduced to a large number of his close family who also happened to be out drinking. Now I'm going to put this in as PC a way as I can, and I don't mean to offend anyone with this... but Simon was the campest, gayest person I'd ever met. Photo Memory Girl, in her infinite wisdom, waited until Gay Simon went to the toilet on Friday, and decided to tell his entire family "Not to worry," because she'd made it her life's aim to "Straighten him out for them."

Upon finding this out, Simon really didn't know what to say to her. She'd claimed to be bi-sexual a number of times – I suppose some women will say anything in an attempt to make themselves appear more appealing to men – but obviously missed the hypocrisy of trying to turn a gay man straight while talking about her own same-sex promiscuity. He decided not to say anything to her about this but without a doubt, this was the point at which their conversations became more strained. All of this stirred up memories of a moment where my love life and work life crossed, back in 2004.

*　　　*　　　*　　　*　　　*

I was working part-time in a sleepy little cinema whilst at university, and I'd gone to work as usual one evening. For reasons unknown to me at the time, the cinema was unusually busy and, for once, I was actually having to do some work. A normal day at work for me had previously meant sitting in one of the big screens, watching a film to ensure no one was smoking or talking, and almost always ended up with me setting my phone alarm on vibrate to let me know when the film was about to finish, allowing me to have a nice nap for an hour and a half. But on this particular day I was running around like a headless chicken, mopping up spilt drinks, sweeping up popcorn, and all these other things which I suppose are done every day by members of staff in cinemas across the land.

After a while it all began to quieten down and an elderly couple approached me at the top of the escalator where tickets are torn. They explained to me that the largest cinema in town had closed that night, due to a power cut, and that's probably why we were busier than usual. I asked them what film they were coming in to see and they said they hadn't decided yet, and wondered if I'd be able to give them a quick tour of the place before they decided if this was going to be the cinema of choice for them that evening, as there were a number of small picture houses in the area. So I got someone to cover for me at the GSP (I hate acronyms – this one stood for General Service Point) and I showed this couple – probably in their early 70s – around the cinema. I was thorough; I even let them go into one of the big screens where a film was playing so they could see the quality of the sound and picture before making their decision as to which cinema to go to.

After my ten-minute tour they thanked me, obviously very grateful that someone had made that effort for them, and went on their way, only to return a few minutes later with tickets for their film of choice. I thought to myself what a lovely old couple they had been. They seemed genuinely impressed and grateful that I'd gone above and beyond the call of duty to show them around. They were just the kind of people who might write a letter of gratitude to the cinema manager, praising him for his wonderful staff.

A few weeks passed at work and nothing exciting happened, and my mind kept wandering back to this couple. I think I need to point out that at this point in my life I was drinking fairly heavily so my rationale was perhaps not what it is now. I found myself actually getting angry that this elderly couple hadn't bothered to write a letter in to the cinema about how awesome I was at my job...

So I decided to write the letter myself.

28

I addressed it from one of my friends who lived nearby in case the letter got a reply, and sung my own praises about my outstanding service, only just stopping short of saying I was the greatest human being ever to walk the earth. I shoved it in a postbox with much satisfaction, hoping that the cinema would recognize what was probably the single greatest contribution anyone had ever made to the film industry.

Like I said, I'd been drinking. As a student my day consisted of getting up at 8am, drinking some Strongbow from the fridge next to my bed, in order to combat the hangover from the night before. Then I'd go into uni, attend a few lectures (through which I tried to get some sleep, then photocopied the notes from my friends later), then go into the studio. Here I would sit and draw, or paint, or make films until about 5pm, when I'd grab something quick to eat and head up to the cinema for work. Then when I finished at 11pm, I went straight out to a club to get extremely drunk, before heading home at about 5am, ready to start the whole process again three hours later. I kept this up for four years, and I'm surprised I didn't die as a result.

So anyway, with the letter written it was just a case of sitting back and waiting to reap the rewards of my hard work. Only it never happened. Had the letter been lost in the post? Was it worth the risk of sending a second letter? I decided against writing again, just in case the letter had fallen into someone's in-tray and hadn't been read yet, but I was getting impatient. I wasn't enjoying working in the cinema and as I'd worked in two other cinemas previous to this one, I could see it for the comparative dump it was and I wanted to get out of there. One day a toilet had backed up and there was... excrement, let's say. All over the floor. The manager politely requested I clean it all up, and I just as politely declined. So suddenly I was facing a disciplinary for refusing to do something which was in my contract (even though they had cleaners to do such jobs), but I stood my ground, determined that under no circumstances would I be cleaning up anyone's poo when I was only getting paid minimum wage. I was nearing the end of my degree so I decided it wasn't worth the hassle of waiting for them to do an investigation into why I'd said no to a manager, and I handed in my notice, to finish the following week. By this point I'd pretty much forgotten about the letter I'd sent, and focused on finishing all my uni work off for its upcoming deadline.

Then, one day shortly thereafter in the uni studio, I met a girl called Violet. She was quiet and shy, and quite attractive. At this point in my life I was painfully shy too, and it took me a week or so to build up the courage to ask her out. What you also have to bear in mind is that at this time in my life, I was a 22-year-old with a mullet. A MULLET. Never a good look, but I guess no one had the heart to tell me at the time. So this sweet girl had to tolerate this blundering, mop-haired idiot coming over, asking her if she wanted to go out for a drink the following night. I was taken aback when she said yes, and I arranged to meet her in the studio the following evening at 6pm. At this stage, you're probably wondering why I'm dragging my love life into this story, but it'll all come together in a minute, you'll see.

The next morning I had a phone call from the cinema I had recently left. Did I owe them some holiday pay back? Had they realized that I used to steal big bags of popcorn when no one was looking? I was relieved to hear... wait for it... that a lovely old couple had written a nice letter to the cinema about what a fantastic customer service experience they'd had. What a surprise! As a gesture of goodwill, even though I'd already left their employ, the cinema's manager wanted me to come to their next staff meeting to collect a £20 HMV voucher, and that their meeting was that night at 5pm.

So off I trundled up to the cinema to collect my £20, with not an ounce of guilt over the fact that I had fraudulently 'earned' this gift voucher. I think my guilt must have been eased by the fact that I actually had been the excellent member of staff that I'd written about in my missive; there was no fabrication other than the names signed at the bottom of the letter. The staff meeting went as usual: A breakdown of sales figures, Team Member of the Month (which funnily enough I was never given, because I was so lazy) and countless other boring corporate things. Then I got called up to the front to collect my voucher, and the letter was read out to everyone (about 60 people). I blushed and made some comment about how I'd always tried to make every customer's experience memorable, then I said my final farewells to the friends I'd made at the cinema and went on my merry way. As I got outside the cinema I turned my phone back on and almost wet myself with woe. The staff meeting had dragged on to a colossal two and a half hours so it was now half past seven. The uni where I'd arranged to meet Violet was a good 15-minute walk away so I decided to run. And by run I mean sprint like my life depended on it. I knew before I got there that she would already have gone. I mean, who would wait around for nearly two hours when their date didn't turn up? And sure enough I got there and she was gone. I was gutted. I'd kept putting off asking her out because I was a chicken, and now I'd finally sorted a date out with her, I'd stood her up. By this point the studio was completely empty apart from me, and as I approached her desk, I saw a note on it which read, "I waited for an hour."

After that day, Violet blanked me. I apologised and tried to explain this funny story about why I'd not turned up but it was too late and I was never particularly good at getting events in the right order when telling stories verbally, so I probably just sounded like a weirdo that she was best off avoiding. I couldn't even blame my workplace for keeping me there too long, because I'd only been there to collect a voucher I wouldn't have been given if I hadn't written that misleading letter. I'd like to say that this incident helped me see the error of my ways, and that I should try harder and live honestly, but it didn't. I'm not really someone who learns from my mistakes.

The Script

Day Seven

To be honest, most of the interesting things which happen to you as a Phone Monkey are directly related to the strange people you work with, when you're training to be a corporate telephone answerer. What's most interesting is the shocking web of lies spun by people like Gay Simon and Photo-Memory Girl. After her not-so-shocking revelation that she was bisexual, Photo-Memory Girl decided to tell us all about her love life.

She insisted on telling us about how, within weeks of breaking up with her cheating boyfriend, she'd managed to pull a hunky doorman in town. She went to the toilet at one point so we decided to quiz Gay Simon about what else had happened on his night out in town with her the previous weekend. In short: Did the bouncer boyfriend exist?

Gay Simon took great pleasure in discussing the weekend's events with us, and how Photo-Memory Girl had talked to a bouncer who was stood outside a club. Apparently she'd been trying to make conversation with him. After less than a minute of conversation, the bouncer had said he had to go back inside to do something but that he would come out and see her in a few minutes. They waited for half an hour and he never came back out, and the other bouncers refused to let her into the club to find him.

Guess that solved that mystery!

*   *   *   *   *

I figure now is probably the right time to fill you in now on a little bit more background on one of my previous occupations. As I've previously mentioned, I was self-employed for longer than I've ever held onto a job: Three years. My decision to go self-employed was based primarily on one factor related to work: I absolutely loathe anyone telling me what to do. You'll understand as this Phone

Monkey story goes on that the kind of inane nonsense that companies make you do, often for illogical reasons, really winds me up something rotten. I was working as an accountant at a school just prior to my self-employment, although that's not entirely true as I don't have any accounting qualifications, and they certainly weren't paying me accountants' wages. There were four of us in the office, one of whom was a miserable old witch who made every effort to point out all the things I was doing wrong, without telling me how to correct my mistakes; another who was only about nineteen but who had lofty ambitions of one day taking my job; and another who was a free-love hippie-type called Natalie who I actually got on with, but rarely got to talk to as she sat at the opposite side of the office. Being stuck in a work environment where you find yourself developing hatred for those around you is not a healthy place to be, so I'd decided that I needed to be finding something else to do with my life within the next few months, before I went crazy and started chopping my colleagues up with an axe.

I was having a conversation with Natalie one lunchtime, and she told me how she used to run a sandwich shop, so I asked her all sorts of questions about being self-employed and all the things that came with it; Tax Returns, keeping accurate accounts, buying stock, etc. It was at this point that I decided, perhaps foolishly, that I could do this. Over the previous twenty years I'd amassed quite a sizeable book and toy collection (don't judge me please), and figured that selling my collection would be a good way to raise some cash to buy some stock (even more books and toys) to set up my own business. And it went well. Really well. For a short time I was earning a lot of money, eventually earning enough to wave a not-so-fond farewell to the accounting job, right at the end of the tax year, knowing full well that due to my general lack of interest in the job, I hadn't been filing things away properly, or keeping full records of all the receipts and invoices that had passed over my desk in the last few months. If the nineteen-year-old wanted my job so badly, she could have it, and good luck with filing that tax return, princess.

Once self-employed I had all the time in the world, and I put it to really good use: By doing virtually nothing for about six months. I was spending most of my nights in town, drinking with friends, then getting up in the morning very much the worse for wear, watching a few films, then going out again the next night. I'm known among my friends as someone who gets myself into ridiculous situations that could very easily be avoided by anyone with an ounce more sense than me, just by saying no to that fatal thirteenth beer.

For my leaving do for the accountancy job, I drank way too much wine... seven bottles in total, all by myself. For some people this will sound like a hell of a lot of wine to get through. To my friends, they'll tell you that's a standard amount for me. I'm not telling you about it in a boastful way - alcohol is evil kids, you need to avoid it at all costs – but I do have an exceptionally high tolerance for it. After all my work colleagues (I won't call them my friends) had left, I wandered into a local pub where a friend of mine was the DJ. It was on this night, back in early 2008, that the "Monkey Special" was invented. This is basically where you go to the bar and order a bottle of wine (the cheapest they have) and a pint of lager (again, the cheapest available) and have a mouthful of lager, then a mouthful of wine (drunk straight from the bottle of course... if you're at the point where you think lager and wine are a good mix, then you clearly won't be bothered about what people think of you drinking the wine straight from the bottle). When you've finished both drinks, head back to the bar and repeat until unconscious.

I managed to spill wine all over my friend's laptop which he was using to DJ, and when he asked me if I wanted a taxi home, I told him I was fine walking, before setting off in entirely the wrong direction. The following morning I woke up, sat up in bed and realised that there was blood all over my bedsheets. I looked at my hand, and all my knuckles were skinned and bleeding. I stood up to go to the toilet, still wondering what had happened, and found my pillow similarly puddled with my own blood. I had a deep gash in the side of my head, and a very painful gravel-filled graze on the back of my head. I had various scuffs and bruises to my knees too, and for a good few hours until my memory started returning, I had no idea what had happened to me. Somehow I'd managed to stagger home from town, and right up until the point at which I got to my front door, I had miraculously managed to survive the night injury-free. Then when I'd tried to get my key in the door, I'd struggled quite a bit. In fact, I couldn't stand upright at this point, and kept falling over, banging my head on the low wall separating mine and the next-door neighbour's garden, at least four or five times. I'd then tried hammering on my own door for someone to let me in (hence the bloody knuckles), before eventually realising that I lived alone. I fell over a few more times, managing to crack my head on the gate, and falling into my gravel-garden, and then managed to turn the key in the lock and I was home. This is why I should not drink. Ever. Especially "Monkey Specials".

I'm not sure exactly how I digressed into my drinking stories there, but anyway, back to the self-employment. I decided to buy 120,000 books, as you do. To anyone normal that might seem like quite an unusual purchase. For me it was just par for the course, and for the next two years my house (and my parents' garage) was absolutely packed to the rafters with them. I made a very good profit on them.

Shortly thereafter, the financial crisis struck and suddenly no one had the money to buy books and toys, so I branched out into selling items which had been returned to big retailers like Argos, which I bought by the pallet and sold individually, again on eBay. The writing was on the wall though. Profits were declining and my outgoings were very quickly becoming greater than my income. So I got the Phone Monkey job, and within a few weeks, boxed up all my books, toys and assorted junk, and sold them in one job lot, to someone who got the bargain of the century. I just wanted my house back by this point, to be honest. Pretty much every room in the house was full of boxes of toasters, books and toys, and that's no way to live. Being self-employed was one of the best things I ever did because it allowed me to experience the freedom of being my own boss but, ultimately, if I was ever going to be able to buy my own house and settle down one day, I needed to find real work.

Infidelity

Day Eight

I'd been out the previous night and got a little bit drunk, then laid in bed all night, unable to sleep. I wasn't sure my test at work today was going to go so well. I really did feel like death. But there was Phone Monkeying to be observed and reported so I was going to suffer through it.

The test we had was on the optional benefits you could add to your home insurance. The list was extremely short, only about half a dozen things. It concerned me that they felt the need to give us a separate test on these. How thick must some of the new trainees be if they couldn't remember six benefits, examples of which were Accidental Damage, Personal Possessions (cover for your items when away from home), and Family Legal Protection (Yawn)? Well, I said it was easy… despite her boasting about her photographic memory yet again, Photo-Memory Girl failed it. So did Gay Simon. And at this point we were introduced to Simon's oh-so convenient dyslexia.

Now don't get me wrong, I understand that dyslexia can be a massive problem for some people. Some of my closest friends from when I was growing up had it, and despite them being well-rounded, extremely intelligent people, it was a very real problem when it came to them sitting exams, as the words just turned into a jumble before their eyes. Gay Simon's dyslexia was not like this at all. He could read perfectly well. There'd been times in the last two weeks when we'd all had to take it in turns to read things aloud to the group (I nearly said "class"; this really did feel like being back at school for me), and he'd had no problem whatsoever in reading fluently. But suddenly, when faced with very simple, straight-forward questions that he couldn't remember the answers to, this of course became dyslexia, and when he re-sat these failed tests, our trainer Leanne practically told him the answers. It made me wonder how desperate they were to fill seats with Phone Monkeys when they let idiots like this pass their training.

Then, apparently as some kind of team-building exercise, we did a pub quiz. Not with questions about work, though, just questions about films and music. I'm so glad they had this training programme thoroughly planned out so we could become the best Phone Monkeys possible.

*   *   *   *   *

Talking about Gay Simon failing his test reminded me of a job interview I had a while back. I'd finished university and a distinct lack of funds had meant that I'd had to come from the fantastic night life of the big city I was studying in, back to the tiny little nowheresville that I'd been spawned from, all those years previously. For about six months I managed to convince my mum and dad to let me live with them, for free, as I set to work on illustrating a kids' book that I had lofty aspirations for getting published by a big publisher. So I drew and drew and drew, and printed out my book (called From The Sky for those of you who are interested), and sent copies off to about twenty different publishers. That's when the waiting began. I don't know if it was arrogance or confidence, but I was 100% certain that my masterpieces would be snapped up, and pretty soon I'd be the next J.K. Rowling.

Alas it was not to be, and as rejection letter after rejection letter flooded in, I became a bit disheartened, and rather than just get back behind the drawing board and keep practicing until I was good enough, I decided to pack it all in and get a real job instead. The problem being: My laziness. The only job I applied for was one at the local pub which had just had a bit of an extension to it, and was now calling itself a classy restaurant. It really wasn't though. It was dirty, smoky (this shows how long ago this story is from – people were still smoking indoors), and worst of all, the same regulars were in the pub every single night without fail. It was depressing.

Still, a job's a job, and the place was a two minute walk from my parents' house, so I went in for the job interview and sat down with the manager at one of their sticky tables, and somehow convinced him that it'd be a good idea to give someone as clumsy as me a job carrying hot plates through a restaurant. Within a few days, he'd even promoted me to head waiter, I think more down to the fact that the two waitresses were only 16 and I was 23, than any testament to my serving abilities.

But as I stood up to leave the interview, I reached out to shake the owner's hand, and he looked me sternly in the eye. This was our conversation:

Owner: "You'll have to take that ear piercing out before you start your first shift here."

Me: "Oh right, yeah, health and safety and all that."

Owner: "No, not health and safety... don't get me wrong, I've got nothing against you gays but some of our customers are a bit more... old-fashioned let's say, and they'll take offence at it."

Me: "I'm not gay."

Owner: "You don't have to be ashamed of it, just don't bring your sexuality to work with you."

Me: "Okay."

I'm totally not gay.

I promise.

What a weird interview.

Boo!
I can't believe Simon. He's being so bossy, expecting me to do whatever he says.
It does seem a bit out of order.
But I'm not going to jump behind him to say boo to the goose.
Did you actually graduate high school?

Day Nine

Our mission on this day was to sit next to qualified Phone Monkeys, just like on the open evening I came to before starting the job, listening to them working. I can only presume that making us do this was their way of warning us how complex and antiquated the computer systems were. The main problem behind this kind of training was that the qualified Monkeys whizzed from screen to screen, inputting data and ticking boxes as they went, much too fast for us to be able to keep up and actually learn anything of any value. Normally I wouldn't question doing this as part of our training, as we obviously needed to be aware of the fast pace of the business, and to listen to some of the awkward queries the customers had, but I got the feeling that there was an ulterior motive at work today. Our trainer Leanne, and her assistant, whose name I hadn't managed to catch yet, were both extremely hungover, so basically we were palmed off so they could have a nice day of sitting doing nothing in their training room downstairs.

And such joys, when I returned home from work I had some post from my own home insurance provider. My policy was due to expire, and the renewal price was way higher than the previous year, so I nipped online, found a cheaper quote, and had to phone up to set up a new policy. All those questions they ask you about the age of your property, and all the locks you have on your windows and doors, suddenly all made sense to me, given that we'd been learning about those things in these last two weeks of training. Basically, that 80-page booklet you get sent when you first set up an insurance policy, with all the small print, and those terms that are deliberately there to help you invalidate your own insurance if you ever try to make a claim... I had to understand what every word of that document said, and be able to discuss it in depth with anyone who asked a question about it.

Something that provided a constant source of amusement for me was the customers' ability to get so angry that they were shouting at me down the phone about their motor insurance. I'm going to fill you in on a little bit of information now that may be news to you, or maybe not, depending on how conscious you are of the nefarious schemes played out by big insurance companies. Every year, your car insurance will go up. They know you need car insurance if you're driving in the UK. It's not optional; If you don't have it, you won't be driving anywhere. They also know that most people really can't be bothered with phoning up each year to get a better quote, and will just accept whatever price plops onto their doormat on the renewal date. However, with just one phone call, you could tell a consultant like me that you weren't happy with your price, and suddenly you would discover the much lower price that you should have been offered the first time around!

All you'd have to do is a simple search on a price comparison website, and you'd find dozens of offers that were much cheaper that what you were currently paying. There really is no such thing as customer loyalty any more. The worst part of that is, when you called up for a discount, we'd been told we had to call it a "Customer Loyalty Discount", which caused me no end of grief when we then got the obvious question, "If you value customer loyalty, why did you send my quote out at a higher price when you knew you could do it for less?" At this point I wished I could say, "Because the insurance company tries to rip off as many people as is humanly possible, because they know that most of you idiots will never think of calling for a lower price."

At that point, most rational people would think, "Oh well, it's only motor insurance. If they don't value my loyalty, I'll just go elsewhere and get my insurance with Insurer X for a lower price." However, there's a good ten percent of you who view it slightly differently. You take personal offence at the fact that they're trying to charge you this higher price. It's the worst atrocity ever committed by man and you want someone's blood. How dare they single you out in such a way, and increase your premium by 30%?! You want to speak to a manager. Hell, you want the CEO of the entire company to drive to your house, give you a big hug, then revert your insurance premium back to what it was ten years ago. After all, you've been a loyal customer for the last thirty-five years, and your price should be going down each year, not up, right?!?

These people were what we affectionately referred to as "The Crazies". They shouted in our ears, they invariably never got what they wanted because they didn't know how to ask politely, and then they left, promising that they'd be telling their friends what a terrible service we provided. There's no consoling these Crazies, and you just had to ride the crazy wave until the call ended and you could get back to talking to actual human beings.

Day Ten

I'd managed to catch an earlier bus today, which I kind of regretted, since it meant that I then had to sit with Gay Simon and Jack while they bickered about little things that didn't matter. Simon claimed that he'd been an assistant manager in a McDonald's, where he'd earned £53,000 a year. Jack knew someone who'd worked there, as the actual manager, and he'd only been paid £20,000. Jack loved to poke and prod Simon, and liked nothing more than proving him wrong. But the reason I was glad I came in early was that I got to take part in this little gem, as described in the comic strip on the next page.

For the record, the comic strips in this book aren't entirely fictional. They're either partially or completely based on things people have said, or things we'd discussed that we wished we could say. I just figured that if you were someone who doesn't usually read books (like me), then it's a bit more fun to have some comics mixed in with the text to stop your mind from wandering.

Coma

Things like this were becoming so commonplace that I started writing them down, and they became the basis for this book. I originally started this as 400-character Facebook statuses on my own personal Facebook account, and I was quickly being inundated with comments about the people I was discussing, and a number of people suggesting I turn this into a blog/book/film, which I figured didn't seem too bad an idea, because if I could get a book published, I could probably get out of doing any real work for a good five to ten years as I lived off the royalties, meaning I'd not have to put up with half the nonsense I'd experienced in the workplace, as described in this book!

The most important thing that happened to me today, though, was playing a gig with my band. I got home from work, got changed, and headed out with my guitar and amp, to a pub where I met my bandmates and informed them that some of my team leaders and trainers from work had agreed to come down and see us play.

Now I've been in a lot of bands over the years, from playing guitar in my friend's garage when I was 16, to playing at festivals when I was 23, and then, as I approached 30, I'd developed the itch to join another band, my eleventh so far. I decided long ago that once I reached 27 I'd stop gigging in bands because that was too old to be in an unsigned band. But it's such a buzz playing on a stage in front of people that I just never really stopped, and my current band is the most popular of all the bands I've ever been in.

As I took to the stage to soundcheck tonight with my band, I saw the girls from work walk in. By walk, I mean stagger. It was fairly early in the evening, about 9pm, and they were already wasted. One of my team leaders bounced up onto the stage and asked if she could dance with us while we played our guitars. Then they all decided this would be a good idea. This stage, which only just fit the four of us band members on, was now quickly being swamped with inebriated Phone Monkeys. We had to usher them off the stage before we could start, but our main trainer, Leanne, called me over to come and have a chat. As I went over, she grabbed me and gave me a spine-crunching hug. I'm not really a huggy person. Then she insisted I hug every other person she was out with, including Gay Simon, from our training group. As I did, I felt him squeeze my bum. How totally inappropriate, and totally expected.

As I took to the stage I knew I couldn't let them get away with abusing me like that, so I dedicated our first song to "The Phone Monkey Sluts." I'm not sure it went down so well, but it was all a bit of fun, which hopefully I'd never get pulled up on back at work.

Day Eleven

Despite not yet being fully trained, today I spent an entire day answering phone calls from actual customers. Please be aware that we had a script to read from, but this 'prepared' document didn't even begin to prepare you for the kinds of questions you were likely to be asked. I sold four different insurance products, and I'll be honest, they were so similar that I had no idea if I was providing the correct information or not. But I didn't worry about it, I carried on, and managed to get through the morning and most of the afternoon without any real panicky moments. The first two calls were somewhat nerve-racking for me and virtually everyone else in the group who'd never done this kind of work before, but after the first half hour, our nerves subsided and we got into the idea that since this was going to be our full-time job for the foreseeable future, we'd best just get on with it and quit whining.

I spent my dinner hour contemplating all the things I'd forgotten to say on calls, and all the mistakes I was aware I'd made. I was worrying I'd spend this evening reflecting on how badly I'm going to screw this company up for The Man. Then, late that afternoon, the bombshell they hit us with was, "We've listened in to some of your calls, and graded you, the same way you'll be graded once you start work up on the floor properly." I'd failed my monitor-thingy. I felt awful. Then I looked around and saw all the sad faces. We'd all failed. I'd never taken so much delight in other people's misery until this day, but I decided this was okay, since I had suffered the same fate as them. We got a mini-roasting, and within ten minutes they'd put us back on the phones to deal with more unsuspecting customers, who mistakenly believed that we had the ability to renew their insurance policies without royally messing them up. I was at risk of invalidating people's insurance and accidentally increasing the prices tenfold!

Anger Management Dept.

Day Twelve

The day had started well. Some more of our calls had been listened to… and we'd all passed. I'd doubted that their "learn while you do the job" method of training would work, but it looked like it had so far. We all still needed to ask for advice or answers to complex questions sometimes, but for the most part we were all plodding along happily without too many problems. The downside to our newly-found independence was that now our three trainers were using their spare time to discuss a variety of weird and wonderful subjects, whilst still in our earshot, when we were trying to concentrate on what the customers were saying to us in our headsets.

The worst one today was when they all pulled up chairs to have a supposedly whispered conversation, to which I heard every word quite clearly. I was even a little concerned that the customers I was talking to may have heard too. Their chosen topic: Viagra. Great. Apparently all three of them had either husbands or boyfriends who had, at some point, experienced erectile dysfunction and had needed some assistance from their little blue friend. They even went into details of "how much longer they'd been able to go for".

Gay Simon thought it would be a good day to introduce us (not in person, just with words) to his stepdad. Apparently he's an angry, hate-filled Nazi, racist, homophobe. Or that's how Simon described him to us. On telling us how he had to move out of his mum's house when he was 16 because of his stepdad's homophobic bullying, he also then ventured onto telling us about a previous job he'd had at another call centre. We couldn't believe the following lies that fell so effortlessly from his lips, but give it a go yourself, and see what you think.

"When I worked for the phone company, there was one manager who always refused to talk to me. I'd go to him with a problem or a question and he'd always tell me to go away. It got to the point where I thought I'd done something wrong so I asked another team leader what his problem was. I was told that the manager was a former army general who had strong anti-gay feelings.

"I confronted him about this and asked him to at least dignify my questions with a response. The manager said that everything about me made him feel sick to his stomach and that he didn't see why he should deal with gays on a daily basis. He refused to help me at all so I asked him to put into writing why he was being so nasty to me. Half an hour later he'd presented me with a piece of paper outlining all the reasons he hated everything I stood for as a gay man. I took this straight to the managing director of the company, and by the end of the day, the homophobic manager had been sacked."

For one second - one foolish second - I believed what he was saying. Then I woke up. From this point on, it became obvious that Gay Simon lived in some bizarre dream world where outrageous things happened on a daily basis, usually with the Hairspray soundtrack playing in the background.

It became mine, Claire, Clive and Jack's new source of amusement: seeing how far Gay Simon's lies would go. He liked to make out that he had a terrible childhood. I'd always thought stupid people had good childhoods, because they were too dumb to realise what they were missing in life through their lack of intelligence. Apparently, not so with Simon.

His next story involved his last day of working for a telecommunications company. His team had gone on an "Away Day" which was basically an excuse for ten people to get slightly drunk and do fun things. Although "fun things" has a different meaning when organised by managers. It involves team-building exercises like that thing where you let yourself fall backwards, to be caught by the rest of your team in a trust-building exercise. This is what he told us about his day out:

"Everything was going great. We'd gone out for a meal and a drink, then went go-karting. Then when we got back they got us all sat round a table, and told us we were going to have an afternoon of karaoke, but with nursery rhymes. I found it all a bit strange, seeing my workmates singing Humpty Dumpty and Incy Wincy Spider. So when it came to me, they told me that I had to sing I'm A Little Teapot. I told them I don't feel comfortable with singing in front of an audience (although I did audition for The X-Factor last year), and they started heaping the pressure on. Eventually they'd got a little chant going. "Simon! Simon! Simon!" But I refused to sing. The manager of the company came in and asked what all the noise was about, and when the guy organising the Away Day told him about my refusal to sing, he said, "Where's your team spirit, Simon? That's just not acceptable. You're fired!"

Take from that what you will. Then pity me for having to sit in a room with this buffoon for five days of every week.

The What?!

Day Thirteen

I got up a little earlier that morning, and rather than have my traditional mountain of fruit, instead I opted for some meat-free falafel. I'm not sure what falafel is, but it tastes like powdered cats.

Tomorrow we would start 'The College', which would basically just be us doing our Phone Monkey duties on the shop floor, with some bizarre name to make us feel a little bit special. I doubt many of the people working in the call centre had ever attended a real college. For today though, there were a few other surprises in store for us. I went for my usual coffee from the machine, and walked past a young gentleman who was sat behind a table with a big sign saying "If I raise £500 I'll shave off my beard and all my hair." I don't know where he got his hair cut but I think he should consider somewhere cheaper if he was getting charged that much. Walking back to our training room, I passed a cake stand and a shoe stall. What was going on?!

When I got into the training room everyone seemed excited, far too excited considering they were in the workplace. I asked what was happening, and Milfy Claire asked me if I'd seen Mystic Mike yet. I pinched myself to see if this was just some kind of bizarre dream but no, there was actually someone called Mystic Mike in the building, and I got the feeling that we weren't going to get much work done today, until we'd all ventured out to see him and shake his mystical hand.

Our trainers had no problem at all with us spending the first hour of our shift in the lobby of the building getting tarot readings from a balding middle-aged man who, as far as we were aware, normally worked here as a Phone Monkey. He came out with the kinds of classic lines which I always associate with these supposed psychics, like "I can see change coming in the future," and "You've been having a hard time lately." What I wasn't prepared for was the fact that most of our group, and our trainers, actually believed all this hokum. Really? I'm going to experience change at some point in the remaining fifty years of my life? Oh, my! How did you know? And this hard time I'm having? It's called life! Oh dear. How gullible some people can be.

I'd hoped that would be the end of it, but our trainers had the bug now, and wanted to follow through with a bit of a Google search. They wanted another psychic to come out and do personal readings on all of us, and possibly try to speak to some dead people while they were at it. After five minutes of them searching unsuccessfully, I had to point out to them that 'Physics' was a science, and 'Psychics' were what they should actually be looking for. I wasn't encouraging them mind you, I just wanted this misery to end as soon as possible, and people not being able to spell basic words is something of a bugbear of mine. I'd be very disappointed in myself if I read this book back one day and found any spelling mitsakes.

Recently, Milfy Claire's dad had passed away, and she was getting excited at the prospect of meeting someone who could put her back in touch with him so she could discuss things she felt had been left unsaid following his sudden death. Now, don't get me wrong, I'm very open-minded, but these people are just taking your money and treating you like an idiot. They're well-trained conmen, telling you exactly what you want to hear in order to give you some kind of catharsis. I think it's morally wrong, although I know for some people it may put their mind at ease.

Photo-Memory Girl had been depressed all day since her encounter with Mystic Mike, as he had told her "Hard times were coming", and that "Love would be cruel throughout her life". If you saw Photo-Memory Girl's face, you too would offer the same feedback on her future love life. Needless to say, I didn't have my future read.

Having discovered that there were no local psychics who could come out to our workplace that day, the whole thing fizzled out (thankfully) and we were finally able to start work.

The Wrong Department

Day Fourteen

We discovered the process for booking holidays, which is actually remarkably straight-forward. The only problem being that trying to find a day that they'll let you have off is nigh-on impossible. Not to worry, I booked myself in for the next available holiday, and I know now that I'll be able to spend my 67th birthday on a beach somewhere. But only for two days, and then I have to be back at work.

As promised, The College was unleashed on us. We were still taking calls the way we were in the training room, only sat with the qualified Phone Monkeys, doing the job in a very noisy office environment. They were also listening in to more of our calls than usual, probably hoping we'd fail so that they could make us feel even less significant than we did already.

Over lunch Gay Simon was telling us about the new house he'd just bought, and how every room was huge. He was decorating it over the next few months, and took great pleasure in telling us how he'd bought a 23 metre mural (I've got to be honest, he kept calling it a Murial), that would go all the way round the bedroom. Apparently they weren't in when the postman tried to deliver it the other day, and his boyfriend Little Rob had gone to pick it up from the sorting office and was going to meet Gay Simon at our workplace to show him the huge artwork. He was very excited.

We finished our lunch and Gay Simon disappeared as expected, only to return a few minutes later with a glum look on his face. We asked him what was wrong.

"Well, I ordered my murial and it got shipped here from Japan, and it cost me a fair bit, but I think I might have read the eBay listing wrong. It has to be my dyslexia playing up again." (Does dyslexia "play up"? I thought it was a permanent thing…)

"I was certain it said 23 metres on the listing, but it's arrived and... well..."

At this point he reached into his man-bag and pulled out an A4 envelope. He slid something out of the envelope.

"It turns out it didn't say 23 metres. It said 23 centimetres. This is it."

He showed us a very finely detailed print of a boat on a river with trees swishing in the autumn breeze. It wasn't even as big as an A4 sheet of paper. We couldn't stop laughing.

"You can't laugh!" he spluttered. "It cost me eighty quid!"

Free Gift

Day Fifteen

After more tedious Phone Monkeying, we headed out for dinner together. As we waited for our first course, Photo-Memory Girl told us how she was on a really strict diet of just vegetables and fruit. That's how she managed to stay so slim, apparently. We all looked at one another. She wasn't slim at all. Had we misheard? Then she told us how she'd been having kick-boxing lessons for two years, and that all the exercise was keeping her "tight and toned". If you saw her, the insanity of her saying that would be obvious. She was, at best guess, an XXXXXXL. I didn't believe for one second that she did any kick-boxing. I quizzed her about it, as I used to do kick-boxing myself, and it turned out she didn't know anything about it at all. Strange that, for someone who claimed to have been doing it for two years.

*   *   *   *   *

Back in 2005, when I was working part-time in a library. I'd just moved out of my parents' house, and a friend of mine, David, was a kick-boxer and decided to teach me a few moves before I joined a class properly, just to see if I was into it before I spent any money. I learnt some basic moves, and I was actually quite fast and fit at this time of my life (long before my beer belly took hold). He took me aside one Saturday morning and said, "I think you're ready to try a fight now. I'll get in the ring with you."

So for a good twenty minutes I kicked and jumped and ducked and dodged, proud of my level of fitness and the fact that I'd survived this long against someone who'd been kick-boxing since he was a child. Then he decided to shatter my little fantasy and told me he'd been going easy on me as he didn't want to risk hurting me. I told him it'd be okay, I needed to know what it would be like to be in a proper tournament, and that he shouldn't hold back. One solid kick from him later, I was sat in the hospital waiting room with broken ribs. It got me six weeks off work though, on full sick pay, so I shouldn't complain really.

*   *   *   *   *

Back at our staff lunch, Photo-Memory Girl's food arrived. She had a prawn cocktail, A steak dinner, and a slice of chocolate fudge cake for dessert. Hmmm, where were the healthy vegetables she mentioned? Clive couldn't finish his dessert, so of course she had to finish it for him. I was so glad her diet was going well.

Later, back on the phones, we were told that we had to split into two teams. Whenever this happened, I always ended up being partnered up with Gay Simon and Photo-Memory Girl, and today was to be no exception. Clive, Claire and Jack were virtually guaranteed a win in this upcoming competition as they didn't have the "Not-Quite Dyslexic" Gay Simon and "There's Not Enough Snack Machines In The Building" Photo-Memory Girl to hinder them.

Things were looking up at first, as the competition involved a prize for the team who sold the most Travel Insurance policies, and I had become well known for the speed with which I could deal with calls. If they weren't interested in signing up there and then, it was "Bye-bye, call back when you've made your mind up," and if they were interested I whizzed through their payment details and got straight on with the next call. I was starting to find that I was quite good at this job, and as of today we were earning bonus for any sales that we made, which gave me all the more incentive to succeed.

My new team leader, Rachel, came over within about an hour of the competition starting. She was surely there to congratulate me on my number of sales. Instead she asked me to log off my phone and go into the office with her. Oh no. That didn't sound good!

Apparently, yesterday on a call, a customer said they couldn't afford to pay for a full year's car insurance in one go, and I suggested that he could pay monthly if he wanted. I hope, like me, you're thinking, "There's nothing wrong with that." The thing is, because I mentioned paying by installments before the customer asked if that was an option, then in the eyes of the Financial Services Authority it looked like I was trying to con the customer into signing a credit agreement with us. So I was getting into trouble for trying to help out a customer who couldn't afford his insurance, and didn't know he could pay monthly!

Whenever a Phone Monkey failed one of these monitors, they listened in to the very next call the Phone Monkey took, to ascertain whether it was a one-off mistake. Unfortunately, on the next call, they said I did the same thing again, which struck me as strange, because I only remembered saying that on the one occasion. But because I had been doing things that meant the business could incur fines from the FSA, they deemed me "A threat to the business" and had me pulled off the phones straight away. I would face a disciplinary hearing tomorrow morning where, in all likelihood, I would lose my job for gross misconduct. Seriously.

Slightly disheartened to say the least, I went and sat back at my desk, where I had to plug my headset into Claire's phone and just listen to her taking calls, as I clearly couldn't be trusted. The end was coming. I'll be honest, it wasn't the threat of losing my job that bothered me so much, it was the fact that I'd spent a good two hours writing this book each night, and it would all have been for nothing if I were not even able to finish the training.

Clive, Jack and Claire all consoled me, telling me that they also didn't know we could lose our jobs just for offering a different payment method. We all found the rules and regulations here very restrictive, and after all those times I thought Photo-Memory Girl or Gay Simon would be the first to leave, I was about to be proven wrong. It was made even worse by the fact that those two grinning hyenas were so smug about it. "Well, isn't it obvious? They incur a 5% credit charge to pay monthly, so it's like you're stealing that extra money from them if you convince them to pay like that." Some choice words came into my head but I decided to restrain myself.

Another half an hour passed, and I got called back into Rachel's office. She had tears in her eyes this time. Was it about to get worse? She sat me down and this is what she said:

"First of all, I want to apologise for what's been said to you today, about the threat of losing your job, and how you weren't doing your job properly. As soon as I spoke to you, I dragged up the files of those two calls you failed on, and listened to them myself. On the first call, there's no question, you tried to convince the customer to pay monthly, and that is a definite no-no. That call was definitely a fail and there's no overturning that one.

"However, I listened in to the second one, and I don't know if they're on smack or something in the monitoring office, but they've gone and pulled up exactly the same call again and listened to it as though it were a different call. I let them know this, and they listened to the next chronological call, and it was absolutely fine. It was a straight-forward renewal and you didn't make a single mistake on it. I've been down to the monitoring office now to find the woman responsible for making such a massive mistake and ripped her a new one. She won't make that kind of mistake ever again, believe me.

"The long and short of it is this: You won't lose your job tomorrow, there won't be a disciplinary hearing, and you can go straight back on the phone now. I'm so, so sorry this has happened, and believe me, I fought your corner and the manager has been made well aware of the errors made by the monitoring team today."

Rachel was still shaking. She was so angry at how incompetent the monitoring team had been, and I was impressed with how much she let it get to her, when I was just another of the hundreds of trainee Monkeys she must train up every year.

I sat back at my desk, quickly told everyone what had happened, then got on with my day. As it turned out, I had an absolutely outstanding day on the phone after that, probably spurred on by what seemed like a minor victory over the monitoring team, and by the end of the day, Gay Simon, Photo-Memory Girl and I had won the competition for the most policies sold, although we only won by one save. If I'd been off the phone for a minute longer, we might not have won. We were each rewarded with a big tin of chocolates, which I was sure I'd devour that night, diet be damned. The highs and lows of this job were staggering. At 3 o'clock I was anticipating being fired tomorrow morning, and by 4 o'clock it was all okay and I was named top salesman on the team.

The following day was dress-down day for some charity or other, so I was considering going to work in my onesie.

Hold Music

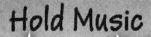

Hi there, Phone Monkey speaking. How can I help today?

Well, last week my boyfriend surprised me with a trip to Las Vegas, where he proposed and we were married by an Elvis impersonator.

It was brilliant. It was the holiday of a lifetime. I suppose I should say the honeymoon of a lifetime! We played in the casinos, went on long romantic walks... It was definitely a trip I'll never forget. I'm calling today to change my name over into my married name.

Well, thanks for telling me that heartwarming little yarn, but unfortunately you're through to the wrong department. You need to speak to Amendments. I'll put you through to them now. Sadly, you'll have to wait in a queue to speak to them.

I'd join the queue on your behalf and call you back when I got through, but the music they play while you're on hold is frightfully depressing and often makes me contemplate suicide. I'll be honest with you, I've got a family at home who need me so it's a risk I'm just not prepared to take. Good luck... and goodbye.

Day Sixteen

For the first half of the day, all six of us and ten people from another training group were taken off the phones. We thought that either a) we'd done something wrong, or b) someone had done something really good and they wanted to share it with all of us. Turns out it was neither. Today, for reasons unknown to me, we'd been picked to take part in four hours of Visual Management. Snazzy job title, yeah?

Sadly, what it actually meant was that the company was doing some kind of Spring promotion and they wanted a display putting up on the walls, with cut-out paper grass, blue tissue-paper skies, some laminated fluffy bunnies and for reasons I'll never fathom... a twelve-foot sheep. They took sixteen of us off the phones, for 4 hours each, to stick pictures on the wall. To say the managers of the call centre were constantly moaning about staff shortages, I don't know whose bright idea it had been to do this, given how much it must have cost for 16 of us to be off the phone for so long, but I hope the responsible manager gets fired and I never had to do anything like this again.

In my free time I occasionally did commissions of artwork for people. Banners for restaurants, stand-up signs for conventions, family portraits and all that kind of stuff. The work was quite sparse but it paid about ten times the hourly rate of what I earned as a Phone Monkey. I wasn't about to tell the managers about my artistic qualifications and create more work for myself as an organiser of this Spring display, so I just kept quiet, doing the tiniest amount of work possible.

In the afternoon I got a telling off, for making a typo on someone's policy. When we added a discount code we had to also type DISC, for Discount, so anyone going into the policy at a later date would know which department made the most recent change on there. Instead I'd just put DIS, and while this code made absolutely no difference to the policy price, and the code DIS didn't relate to any other department anyway, they still pulled the dunce's cap onto my head and made me stand in the corner facing the wall for an hour.

Our frustration about the lack of holiday availability continued as Gay Simon decided to have a shouting match with Jack about it. It was quite comical to watch, especially the outcome so here's what was said:

Gay Simon: They've got to let me have the 10th of August off work. They can't stop me.

Jack: Why, what's happening then?

Gay Simon: It's Gay Pride in town.

Jack: I totally get that you're gay, but why does that mean you get the day off work?

Gay Simon: You wouldn't stop religious people going to their church or mosque, would you?

Jack: Being gay isn't a religion though.

Gay Simon: You're just being homophobic now. I can't talk to you when you're being like this.

Jack: Like what? I'm just asking what everyone's thinking! I don't feel the need to go and march for Straight Pride when I should be at work. Your sexuality shouldn't be an issue, whatever it is. And it certainly shouldn't be affecting your work or letting you get time off.

Gay Simon: It's people like you that repress us gays.

He then took off his headset, threw it down on the desk and minced off. Our trainer, Rachel, couldn't believe he'd just walked away from his phone when it was still logged in. A call could have come through at any second. Something that's only really come to mind now, at the thought of Gay Simon mincing off, is the fact that he always walked a bit weird and stiff, like he'd pooed himself or something. I'm not sure why that's relevant to this story, but I thought you might like to know anyway.

*   *   *   *   *

Speaking of unprofessional conduct, in 2002 when I was working in a cinema, one of my best friends, Hugh, called me to invite me to his leaving do, as he was jetting off to Canada for 6 months as an exchange student. I'm not one to miss a party, but given that I was scheduled to work that day, I had no way of getting out of it, and resigned myself to the fact that I wouldn't be able to say goodbye to him before he went.

Then it struck me: I got a 45-minute break, and Hugh's house was a 20-minute walk from the cinema. I could get there, say my goodbyes (If only for five minutes), then get back to work. So off I went, and as I got to Hugh's house I made the fatal error of accepting a nice glass of red wine. All our friends were there and it was difficult to not let myself get caught up in the party mood. He'd been telling people about a song he and I had written together, and of course everyone wanted to hear it. He got the guitars out and we played the song, and someone else handed me another glass of wine. It'd be rude to turn down free wine, wouldn't it?

There was a good selection of sandwiches, cakes and crisps, so I tucked in. Hugh and I played a few more songs, and suddenly I'd drunk two bottles of wine. Then someone said, "Didn't you have to be getting back to work?"

I didn't run back to work, but I certainly walked fast. My 45-minute break had become a 3-hour break and as I entered the cinema, I prepared myself for the massive telling-off I was sure to get. I went back behind the concessions stand and started serving customers, painfully aware of the fact that I was absolutely wasted, and I was sure to be fired for my actions that break-time.

But I wasn't. The management were so rubbish that they hadn't even realised I'd been missing, and even when I spoke to them, they never picked up on the fact that my speech was slurred and I couldn't walk in a straight line. It was a very lucky escape.

Photographic Memory Girl Strikes Again

Day Seventeen

At work today the madness continued. Someone called up to cancel their pet insurance, and I told them that it would cost them £24 to cancel, or if they stayed with us for the remaining two months of their policy, for £6 a month, it would work out cheaper for them; half the price in fact. Cue the sirens. Apparently I couldn't tell someone that staying with us as a customer was cheaper than cancelling. I didn't know why, and no one could really explain it to me. It's getting to the point where a customer would ask a simple question and I'd have to sit there thinking, "Am I allowed to answer that?" It's political correctness and obsessive protocol gone mad.

All the fun stories about Gay Simon will have to be put to one side today, as he's taken the entire day off to go to his doctor's to get some pills to help him stop smoking. I've never understood why people who smoke can't just stop. How pleasurable can it really be, breathing in smoke, knowing full well that in about twenty years' time your lungs are going to fall out, and you'll die a slow, painful death? If that isn't incentive enough to quit smoking, I don't know what is. But I was sure Simon would have lots of made-up stories about what happened at the doctor's when we saw him the next day. To be honest, no one really believed he'd gone to the doctor's. We thought he was probably sat at home watching cartoons.

Alan

Day Eighteen

"Where's Gay Simon?" asked our trainer, Rachel. It was a good question. We'd all turned up as usual at half past eight, and he'd sat with us while we waited to start our shift. He'd talked some more nonsense about his hard life as a child, but when it came time to start the shift, he'd promptly disappeared. If there was one thing they were obsessed about there above all else, it's that you were on the phone when you were supposed to be. If you started your break two minutes too early or late, you got in trouble. If you went to the toilet twice a day, you got a polite suggestion that perhaps you might try going in your break times. And heaven forbid, should you ever take a sick day, all hell would rain down on you, and you'd be banished to the naughty step.

I'll come back to what happened to Gay Simon in a minute, but I've just reminded myself of something that happened a few days ago. Clive had called in sick. We'd seen him the day before, and knew he wasn't faking it. He was very ill, and no one was surprised that he hadn't turned up. He'd let work know in plenty of time, and he came back to work the following day, slightly healthier-looking, thanks to a much-needed day of relaxing. What I found out a few days later was that he'd had his back-to-work interview about being off sick, and was told that if he had one more sick day in the first six months of working as a Phone Monkey, they would immediately terminate his contract.

I found it a bizarre policy that if you were sick, no matter how ill you were, you had to come into work. They seemed unaware of the fact that the more ill people you have in a workplace, the more people they can pass the illness to, and the more potential you have for your entire workforce going off on sick leave in one go. They told us that even if you had a bad cough and lost your voice, you should still come into work so they could "find something else for you to do". Fact: They wouldn't. They'd see how ill you were, badger you into doing some time on the phone, then when you'd coughed and spluttered your way through half a dozen customers, they'd ask you if you want to go home, while making it absolutely clear that if you did, you'd be in serious trouble tomorrow.

Gay Simon finally emerged about two hours later, and sat down at his desk looking a bit dazed, and his eyes were red. I asked him if he was okay and he said he didn't want to talk about it. Our trainer, Rachel, told him that he'd have to talk about it, at least in private with her, as he'd missed two hours of time on the phone, so he was in a lot of trouble. He decided to bare his soul to us on his next break:

"I went to the doctor for them pills yesterday, to stop me smoking. I have to take one every eight hours so I took one yesterday afternoon, one last night, and another this morning. The doctor didn't tell me about the side effects though. I've been sat in the toilets for the last two hours, crying uncontrollably. I don't even know why. I phoned him and asked if I should stop taking them, and he said no, this is completely normal! I think I might have to start smoking again because I can't deal with the stress of these pills."

Something came to light today that we weren't aware of at the time. Basically, about a week ago, we had to work on a Sunday because our trainer had booked the Friday off and we couldn't be trusted to do the job by ourselves. But Gay Simon never turned up on the Sunday. When we asked why he hadn't made an appearance, he mumbled something about "personal issues" and we left it at that. Today he said that the reason he'd been off was that his grandma had been hit by a drunk driver and he'd had to spend the whole day in hospital with her because no one else cared enough to go and see her, and he didn't want her to, quote, "Die alone". Where this all falls apart is the fact that if you checked his Facebook profile for that day, it quite clearly showed photos of him and Little Rob lounging around in the garden drinking cocktails, with statuses along the lines of "loving the weather, today couldn't be a more perfect day". Oh dear. You'd think he'd realise that if he was going to lie to us, he should at least have covered his tracks.

Adoption

Day Nineteen

Photo-Memory Girl had given her usual "I'm on a diet" speech as she wolfed down handfuls of scones and pancakes. Her head was becoming more orange and pig-like by the day.

We got to listen in to a few of each other's calls today, to see how we were all progressing in different ways. On Gay Simon's calls, he kept making the same mistake when selling motor insurance. Whenever anyone spelt their number plate out to him phonetically, if there was an X involved and they said, for example, Bravo Delta X-Ray for BDX, he would type an E instead of an X. I think he must spell it Ex-Ray. Oh dear. I waited a good five or six calls before telling him because it was too funny to only let it happen once. He blamed it on his imaginary dyslexia again.

Rather than melt our brains by making us learn the full phonetic alphabet, we'd been told that we didn't have to stick to it as rigidly as A for Alpha, B for Bravo, etc., and that we could choose our own words to match the letters. Now this could lead to lots of fun, especially with customers who didn't speak very good English, because it opened the door for us to thoroughly confuse them. I longed for the day when someone's car registration number had the letters PGT in it. "Yes, sir. That's P for Pneumatic, G for Gnome and T for Tsunami.

When we had just started our second week of training, nearly three weeks ago, another team of Phone Monkeys had started as well, in another training group. We'd heard rumours in the last few days that this other team weren't really up to scratch, and that because they were such a large group (19 in all), they were suffering from not having had as much one-to-one time as we had. After all, there were only six in our group so we had been getting preferential treatment. Because of how slow they were learning, and because of some errors made on motor insurance policies which meant that some customers were driving around illegally without insurance, today they fired seven Phone Monkeys in one go. Can you imagine not even being good enough to finish your training in a job before they fired you? How humiliating.

Every now and again I got a customer who was just plain bizarre. This was going to be one of those days. The phone call started out as usual, I asked for her policy number, her name and address and all that hoopla. She was 65 years old, and had called about her travel insurance, wanting to let us know that her husband had suffered a heart attack a few months prior to the call, and wondering if that would affect the cost of her insurance. Sounds straightforward enough, right? Well, this is how it went:

Phone Monkey : Hiya, how can I help today?

Customer : Well, me and my husband are going away in July for a few weeks and I wanted to - - oh, hold on.

(silence for ten seconds)

Phone Monkey : Hello?

Customer : Hi, sorry about that. There was a peeping noise.

Phone Monkey : Oh, okay. How can I help with your travel insurance?

Customer : Yeah, I just wanted to let you know-- oh, hold on again--

(sound of customer fidgeting)

Customer : Can you not hear that peeping noise?

Phone Monkey : No, I can't hear any, uh, peeping.

Customer : Yeah there's a high-pitched peeping noise. Wait there a second. ALBERT!!! COME AND SEE WHAT THIS PEEPING NOISE IS!!!

78

Phone Monkey : Do you want me to call you back later?

Customer : No, it's okay. Albert'll find the peeping noise.

Phone Monkey : I can't hear anything.

Customer : Not to worry. Anyway, Albert had a heart attack a few months back and - - oh no, that peeping's getting louder, I'm surprised you can't hear it - - I just wondered how that would affect his insurance.

Phone Monkey : No problem, I'll put that information into the system and see how it affects the price.

Customer : ALBERT! HAVE YOU FOUND THAT PEEPING NOISE YET?

In the background, presumably Albert: "I don't know what you're going on about woman! I can't hear any peeping noise!"

Customer : I'm really sorry, I'll have to call you back later, this peeping noise is driving me nuts.

Phone Monkey : Okay, bye.

And to be honest, that peeping noise was driving me nuts too, and I couldn't even hear it. How odd.

Those were the kinds of people we had to deal with every day.

*   *   *   *   *

I think now is probably the right time to introduce you to Dribbly Dan. The only problem with Dribbly Dan is that his name kind of gives away his major malfunction as a human being, but I'll fill you in on the details of his life and we'll go from there.

A few years ago I worked in a cinema with Dan who was, for all intents and purposes, "special". Not "special" as in "gifted" or "unique"... come on, you know the kind of "special" I mean.

I came up the escalator in the cinema one day, and there he was, stood at the top, waiting to greet the guests. There was a woman in front of me, who took her ticket up to him, but as she and I approached, we noticed something very odd. Dan was stood there dribbling. Not just a tiny bit in the corner of his mouth. This was full-on pool-of-water-on-the-floor dribbling. This woman stopped for a second, unable to believe what she was witnessing, but then quickly realized she couldn't escape him. She had to approach with her ticket. He reached out for her ticket, and asked her what film she was here to see, while simultaneously spurting a further mouthful of water onto the floor. I had to dive in front of her and grab her ticket to avoid any further humiliation, and I sent her off in the direction of the concessions stand. I reported Dan to a team leader; I'm not a grass, but come on, he was supposed to be the face of the cinema and he was stood there dribbling all over himself and the floor. I ran back behind the concessions stand and found myself apologising for his dribbliness, while giving her free popcorn, and trying to turn it into a humourous anecdote about him being part of the cinema's outreach program.

I'd known Dan for a number of years. I worked with him at Burger King about eighteen months previously. Dan had turned up for a normal shift one morning, worked his eight hours... actually now that I think about it, the idea of Dan serving food to anyone makes a bit of sick come up my throat... anyway, he finished his shift and went in the back to get his coat.

The next morning, 8am rolled around and Dan hadn't turned up for his shift. The manager tried calling him but his phone had died so he had no way of getting in touch with him. The rest of us staff pulled together and did our daily duties without him. He was more of a hindrance than a help to be honest, but all we could talk about was how unusual it was for Dan to be off work.

We finished our shifts, packed up and went home, and the next morning we came in, again surprised to find no sign of Dan. It really was unusual for him to miss any days of work, let alone two in a row. I went in the back room to dig out some bread buns, and when I pulled them off the front of the shelf, I was very surprised, to say the least, to find Dan laying down, right at the back of the bottom shelf. My initial reaction was panic : Was he dead? Who'd put his body there? But then I heard him snore. I fetched the team leader who poked him with the end of a broom (no one dared shake him awake as there were unsubstantiated rumours that he'd once been violent in a nightclub). He woke up and said good morning to everyone, and asked if it was time for him to start his shift. Turned out, he'd climbed onto the shelf to have a quick nap after the end of his shift two days ago, and had only just woken up. Needless to say, for missing his shift, as well as for sleeping in the food area, he was fired on the spot. Poor dribbly Dan.

*   *   *   *   *

At the end of our Phone Monkeying shift today, Photo-Memory Girl was taking great pleasure in telling Milfy Claire about her collection of Mulberry bags. From the sounds of it, she had every design ever created, in every colour available. She also told us that she'd bought a posh flat near to where we work, although for some reason she couldn't move in for six months. We'd let the posh flat slide for once; we knew that her and Gay Simon told lie after lie, but we could at least pull her up on the Mulberry bags as she said she was going to bring two or three of them in to show us all the next day.

£40,000

Day Twenty

Every Thursday and Friday was dress-down day at work. It was very much like a non-uniform day at school, but there were still very strict dress codes in place, like no football shirts, no shorts, no flip-flops, and nothing that even remotely represented anything like having a good time. I felt like an extra in Orwell's 1984 sometimes. Milfy Claire had brought one of her Mulberry bags in, as she did every dress-down day, and as we mingled with a few of the newbies from the other training group before work, all the girls were cooing and aahing at the shiny new bag. I personally didn't understand why people felt the need to spend hundreds of pounds on a handbag, but then again I suppose a lot of people wouldn't understand why I needed more than one electric guitar when I could only play one at a time.

Photo-Memory Girl oinked her way into the crowd, looking for attention as she always did. But where were her Mulberry bags? All she seemed to have with her was her usual manly Reebok rucksack. Milfy Claire decided to confront her about it, and we couldn't believe the outcome.

Claire: I thought you were bringing some Mulberry bags in to show us today? I was really looking forward to seeing them.

Photo-Memory Girl: Mulberry bags? I don't know what you're talking about.

Claire: You said you had loads of them.

Photo-Memory Girl: It wasn't me.

Claire: We only discussed it last night, it was definitely you.

Photo-Memory Girl: You must have me mixed up with someone else. Come on, Simon, are we going out for our customary 57 fags before we start work?

We'd all seen her conversation about the bags the night before so this was very strange.

Still, I had a gig with my band that evening so all I really had to worry about was making sure that I didn't drink too much and have to sit in work the next morning with a hangover.

The New World

Day Twenty-One

Today was the final day of our training. Apparently we'd learnt everything we were ever going to need to know, and we were free to leave the nest and glide through the air on our first solo flight.

Our trainer, Rachel, was sad to see us go, but she had a new training group starting next week, not that I am in any way suggesting that there's a high turnover of staff there or anything.

I hated when things ended like this. The six of us would be going off into our own teams with twelve new names to learn each, and we all had different shift patterns, so it was unlikely we'll ever see each other again. Rachel decided that we should go off and say hello to our new teams, so I was sent over to my new team leader, Elizabeth. She was very loud and opinionated. I sat in their staff meeting with them, got introduced, then all twelve of my new team members promptly ignored me, or if I asked a question about anything, they stared at me like I was an idiot. I could see that working here properly was going to be a lot of fun.

I was going out into the real world to slave away in the battery farm that was the call centre, and I hoped that I wouldn't be here forever.

"Thanks for your call, have a nice day now!"

BOOK TWO:
THE TAKEOVER

Day Three Hundred and Sixty-Six

One year to the day since I started selling insurance, the bosses had big news for us. They'd taken every single consultant off the phone for two hours in all five call centres across the country. Some of us were half-expecting to be told that there were going to be massive lay-offs. Whatever it was, we knew it must have been big news for them to lose over 10,000 man-hours of our work.

I'd love to be able to tell you that the five misfits, who did their training with me, were still here at the insurance company, but sadly they've all gone. All moved on to pastures new. For Clive, Jack and Claire it was simply a case of better job offers coming up, and them moving onto bigger, better things. For Gay Simon, it was disciplinary after disciplinary, all centred around the fact that he spent at least fifty percent of every shift in the toilet, although no one really knew what he was actually doing in there for four hours a day. He'd sign onto the phone, take a few calls, then go off on a toilet break for ten minutes, before taking a few more calls and repeating the same nonsense again and again, until the end of his shift. The higher-ups knew they wouldn't be able to get away with firing him (he'd always play the gay card), so instead they relocated him to London, for him to train up the next lot of newbies in travel insurance. I felt very sorry for those newbies, as Gay Simon's time with the company involved failure after failure, and numerous customers complaining that basic things they'd asked him to do had just not been done. Oh well, he'd gone now. Photo-Memory Girl… well, I'll save her story for a bit later on.

We gathered in the foyer, each of us speculating as to what we might be about to be told, as our manager jumped up onto a makeshift stage that looked about as shaky as the company's pricing structure.

"Okay, I know a few of you have had concerns about today's announcement, but let me put all your minds at ease: We're not laying anyone off. This is good news for the business, not bad. Basically, the company which has been running us for the last five years have decided to sell us and as of right now, we have a new owner. Now this new owner has worked with a lot of call centres in its time and we don't anticipate any major changes to the way we do things. Over the next month or so you'll all be asked to sign new contracts with the name of our new owner on them, but the most important thing, I think, is that your pay and bonus will remain exactly the same. Samantha is going round now, handing out booklets with all the information about the takeover and what it means for you all, and if you have any questions, feel free to come and talk to me at any time."

Immediately following this meeting we were given an hour in our individual teams to discuss this change of ownership, and voice any concerns we had. As part of this announcement, the business had put on a buffet for us. I'm not really sure why. And for the next hour when we should have been discussing the business's future, we ransacked the buffet tables, fighting for sausage rolls, sandwiches, chocolate bars and cans of pop. I don't think anyone actually cared that the business had changed hands; we'd just been told our pay and bonus would remain the same so there was surely nothing to worry about. How foolish we all were.

*   *   *   *   *

Since there's been a bit of a gap between my training finishing and now, I can give you a very brief summary of what you've missed. The woman assigned to be my team leader when I joined the team eleven months ago, Elizabeth, was never around for me to ask for assistance, and after two months we were all told she'd been promoted and we'd get a new team leader. This new team leader, again, was never around and then left the business one month after inheriting us as her team. Not a great start.

Because they were running out of team leaders, we were then assigned a Step-up Team Leader; basically someone who was one of us; a regular Phone Monkey, but who had ambitions of becoming a team leader the next time they advertised the job. Her name was Tina. We were all shocked that she wasn't one of these obsessive "Do everything the way the company demands it" people. She was friendly, helpful, and offered advice where needed. In short, she was not cut out for management-level responsibilities because she sympathised with us Phone Monkeys too much, something the top managers frowned upon. There was a definite "Them and Us" mentality about the head honchos here. As the next lot of team leader interviews came and went, she didn't get the promotion and yet again we were lumbered with another new team leader who, sadly, was about as much use to us as a chocolate teapot.

Goodbye, Old Friend

Day Three Hundred and Sixty-Seven

For some reason, today my breaks fell at different times than those of the other people on my team, and everyone had gone off for their lunch. There was a bit of a gap between calls and my new team leader, Michelle, came over to talk to me. Team leaders coming to talk to you was usually a sign that you'd done something wrong, but this was how it went:

Phone Monkey: What can I do for you?

Michelle: Well, the new bosses have been looking at the stats and they've noticed that when people log off to go home at 5 o'clock there's still calls waiting to be answered, and if we have a certain percentage of calls that go unanswered, we get a big fine so they're not overjoyed about it.

Phone Monkey: Right...

Michelle: So would you be okay staying a little bit later some nights to take those calls?

Phone Monkey: Well, yeah, if it's going down as overtime, that's fine. I could do with the money to be honest.

Michelle: Well, it'd only go down as overtime if you did a full hour of taking calls.

Phone Monkey: So if the calls were all answered by one minute to six I wouldn't get any overtime?

Michelle: That's right.

Phone Monkey: Why would I ever agree to that? I'm not giving up my time for free. That's crazy!

Michelle: Don't you want to help the business out?

Phone Monkey: It's not a case of not wanting to help the business out. It's a case of paying people for the work they do. There's no one in our team that would work potentially for free, in the hope that they might get a full hour's worth of calls and get a bit of overtime.

Michelle: I'm sensing a bit of an attitude problem here.

Phone Monkey: You want me to work for free, at no notice, when you know I car share with someone else here, and would have to rearrange my lift home?

Michelle: I don't think it's a lot to ask.

Phone Monkey: Well my answer's no. If you want to take some calls yourself, feel free. But I finish at five, and that's when I'll be leaving. My contract says if you want to change my hours you have to give me six weeks' notice, and that any overtime is paid.

After that, I was fuming, and as soon as I went on my lunch, I found every single member of my team and warned them what Michelle was inevitably going to ask them. They couldn't believe her gall either. I wonder how many less headstrong people might have just agreed to working for free if they hadn't been warned they were going to be asked?

Shouting Gets You Nowhere

Day Three Hundred and Sixty-Eight

The impact of the new owners hit us today, and hard. Despite their claims of wanting to keep the business running pretty much how it was, they'd suddenly decided to change all our working hours, effective from six weeks' time. We have a choice to make, of which shift we'd prefer, but all the options were so vague and non-committal that no one really knew what they were signing up for, which I guess might have been their plan all along.

Something which I meant to mention earlier was something that I discovered in the toilets. I was a creature of habit and always went in the same cubicle in the toilets to relieve myself, and when I first started there I noticed that a few disgusting creatures had been picking their nose in the toilets and wiping their bogies on the wall. Disgusting, I know. But something intrigued me. There were high ceilings in our building and someone had started flicking their bogies up onto the ceiling in the corner of the toilets. Every day I'd go in there and there'd be more ceiling-bogies. There were now literally hundreds of them. I didn't know why the cleaners hadn't done anything about them. I think one day I'll go in there and the bogie-mural will be complete and there'll be a beautiful bogiefied Mona Lisa smiling down at me.

*   *   *   *   *

On a totally unrelated note, a long time ago, for a very short time, I worked in McDonald's and a sign they had up always made me smile. I'm obviously easily amused, since I'm including it here. I believe this notice is still on McFlurry machines across the UK today:

"Remember : Flurry for eight seconds. It's not a flurry if it's not flurried."

Straight To The Top

Day Three Hundred and Sixty-Nine

How to annoy your workforce: Tell them that their pay and bonus will remain the same with the new management, and then tell them three days later that their bonus is going to be reduced by two thirds.

This happened to us earlier today. The points system used to calculate our bonus based on how many policies we sold had been slashed. We wouldn't know for certain how much our pay would drop by until payday, but as the top bonus-earner on my team, it had been estimated by management that my bonus would drop from £300 a month to £100.

How could they justify it? Well, they didn't have to, did they? They told us it was to help the business through the difficult time of reorganisation as they decided how much of their budget they wanted to spend on staff salaries and bonus. And as one smug manager took great delight in adding, "We don't have to pay you bonus at all, you know. It's a perk of the job and you should be grateful for it."

That was all well and good but even with the reduced bonus included, our salary was barely above minimum wage. The whole reason staff stayed with the insurance company for so long was that their bonus was high and they could earn much more than by getting a similar entry-level job in a supermarket, or as a secretary. I'd effectively just taken a huge pay cut and there was nothing I could do about it.

As if the bonus cut wasn't enough, I got even more bad news today. Earlier in the week Elvis, a Phone Monkey in my team, had okayed it for me to price-match someone's Pet Insurance price with another company's price, and it turned out it wasn't okay to do that at all. The call was listened to and scrutinised by the basement-dwellers, and because essentially I defrauded the company of a few measly pounds, they were going to reduce my bonus by 50% that month. The fact that an assistant team leader approved the transaction didn't seem to matter to those people. I was the one who put the policy through at a reduced price and therefore I was in the wrong. So my bonus wasn't reduced to a third of its normal rate, it was reduced to a sixth. Oh, how I loved working here.

Not that anything could really take away the pain of such a loss in earnings (I struggled to get by as it was, without further money being taken from me), but I tried to stay positive and one of the activities that caused the most amusement among us was a daily competition. Who could get the customer with the most ridiculous name? To take part, at least one other consultant must see the name of the customer on your screen. At the end of the day, the team would pick the winner. Some of my favourites, and I know I'm being childish with some of these, were Mr. Sheepwasher, Mr Dicker and Matthew Matthews. Over the last year I've spoken to at least four different people with the name Mr. Raper, which is surely the most unfortunate name in the entire world. David spoke to Robin Hood, and I spoke to a Muhammad Ali twice. In training, Clive spoke to a Chinese fellow who sounded like he'd be good to take out on a night out with you: He was called Wing Man.

Too Much Like Hard Work

Day Three Hundred and Seventy

As today had been somewhat slow, I'm going to fill you in on what happened to the wonderful Photo-Memory Girl, and the events that led up to her being dismissed.

Three months out of training, she took a call. Nothing out of the ordinary about it; all she had to do was renew someone's car insurance. This was, after all, what we had been trained for, and it could have been done with three clicks of a mouse. She finished the call and the customer, satisfied that his car was insured, went off on holiday to Australia for three weeks, leaving his car parked outside his house.

Upon his return he was a little concerned. His car had gone, clearly the work of thieves taking advantage of his absence. The man called the police immediately, only to be told that his car hadn't been stolen, it had been towed away for not having current motor insurance on it. Understandably, he was furious. His next call was to us, so he could have a bit of a shout at someone, and then get his insurance put back on his car, which was done for him. Then he called the police back to find out where his car had been impounded. They gave him the address, and he had to catch two buses to get there. On his arrival he spoke to a frightened-looking checking-in-and-out guy, who told him, "Oops, it was scrapped yesterday, for not having valid insurance, and for you not coming to collect the car with insurance in place within two weeks of the car being towed."

The car was now a two-foot cube of scrap metal. It was one year old. One further phone call to us, and because of the evidence the customer had (every call made to us is recorded), we agreed that even though the insurance hadn't been set up as he'd been told it would be, we would, in fact, have to pay out to replace his car.

Photo-Memory Girl was dragged into an office by her hair and slapped with a ping-pong bat until she admitted she could have possibly made a small error. She hadn't completed her 6-month probation by that point so, surprise surprise, she was sacked on the spot.

To make things worse, the poor customer spoke to a good lawyer, and our company was then successfully sued for a further £25,000 for the mental anguish imposed on him by the gross negligence on our part. That was not a good day to ask the manager for a pay rise.

On the subject of complaints, I'd had a few made about me over the last year. I tried my hardest to be polite, even to the Crazies, but occasionally I did lose my rag at the idiocy of some people. If a customer told me they were not happy with the price of their travel insurance, I had to offer them a discount, if one was available. It was as simple as that. It was company policy. I even explained this to some customers, usually when there was no discount available, to emphasize the fact that I had done everything I could to fulfill their needs. With the really stroppy ones I even let them know that my job was bonus-based so it was in my best interests to keep every possible customer on our books. If I could have offered them a discount to retain their business, I would have done.

So the next time you call your insurance company and express your dissatisfaction with the price (possibly also mentioning a fictional quote you've had elsewhere at a lower price), and if the consultant then tells you that the price they sent out in the post was their best price, then this is almost certainly the case.

Please don't, as one customer did recently with me, demand to know the ins and outs of every single reason as to why the price of your policy has gone up. Insurance companies just put their prices up. Accept it. Part of this is genuinely down to rising costs in the industry. In car insurance for example, a lot more whiplash claims are being made now than ever before, largely down to American compensation culture infecting our society, so if you're involved in an accident the likelihood of a whiplash claim is increased, and therefore the insurance companies have to charge more so they have enough money in the pot to be able to pay out in this eventuality. The other reason for the price increase is simple: This is business. BIG business. There's a lot of money involved in selling insurance, and if they think they can make a bit more by charging each customer an additional £50 this year, they'll do it. A million customers multiplied by £50 equals a lot of money. If you're not happy, go to another insurer. It's not rocket science. But the conversation with my customer went like this:

Customer: Why has my motor insurance gone up by 40% this year?

Phone Monkey: Changing circumstances in the insurance market have meant we've had to increase premiums in order to be fully prepared for any claims which may be made against the policy. (Please note, this is the company line which we have to read verbatim; I hate vague statements like this.)

Customer: But what specifically has changed? I haven't made any claims or had any speeding convictions.

Phone Monkey: Unfortunately we've had to have a price increase across the board, and the price we've quoted is the best price we can do this year.

Customer: It's gone up £200. I want to pay the same price I paid last year, or less.

Phone Monkey: I wish I could help sir, but this is the best price we can do.

Customer: But why has it gone up so much?

Phone Monkey: Like I said, the changing market means we have to increase the prices.

Customer: But why? Give me some specific examples of what's changed in car insurance that means I have to suffer a 40% price hike?

Phone Monkey: Unfortunately sir, that information is sensitive to the business and we are therefore unable to provide it.

Customer: Look, can you justify to me why the price has gone up?

Phone Monkey: No sir. The price is as quoted on your renewal letter. No one is forcing you to insure with us. If you feel you can get similar cover for a better price elsewhere, it's your prerogative to not renew with us.

Customer: Tell me why it's gone up!!!

Phone Monkey: Changing circumstances in the insurance market.

Customer: Get me your manager. They'll tell me why my price has gone up.

Phone Monkey: No they won't sir. The information is commercially sensitive. They'll tell you the same thing I have.

Customer: Give me a BEEEEEPing reason!!!

Phone Monkey: I'm sorry sir, you're shouting at me now. I'm going to hang up.

Customer: This is BEEEEEPing ridiculous! Get me your---

CLICK.

I hung up on him. I admit that this looks like terrible customer service on my part but what else could I do? I couldn't reduce his price. The company wouldn't let me tell him why his price had gone up, and he'd started shouting and swearing at me. If you're ever caught in this situation as the customer, please don't shout at the consultant giving you the vague information. Every company has its rules and regulations which are monitored, so if the consultant told you that they couldn't give you a certain piece of information, they weren't being difficult: They really couldn't give you that information, no matter how much they wanted to. We had to be honest on every call. We tried very hard to keep all our customers happy, but sometimes there's just nothing we can do about the cost of your insurance or the things we're allowed to disclose to you on recorded calls. Remember: No one's forcing you to stay as a customer with your insurance company.

Six times a month we would get our calls listened to by an elite team of consultants who hid in the basement of the building, because they knew that if they marked us down on calls we lost some of our bonus and if we had easy access to these people, we'd want to beat them to a pulp for being so pedantic. Over the last twelve months it was safe to say that I'd only failed twice on these monitored calls, but even then it was very disappointing to know that they could take 50% of your bonus off you for forgetting to say one line of your script.

Today I failed another one. Every time we failed on something, we listened back to the call, to check if they monitored it wrongly, or missed something that was said on the call. A good 20-30% of the time we could get failed monitors overturned due to an error made by the monitoring consultant. Sadly, today I failed for something that I couldn't contest. About three weeks ago, at the end of my shift, the woman sat next to me, Amanda, finished her shift whilst I was still taking a call, and switched her computer off. Or that's what she thought. What she'd actually done was switch my machine off, right when I was in the middle of renewing someone's pet insurance. I was convinced at the time that I'd done everything I needed to renew that person's insurance, but the computer had obviously not had enough time to save the information, as the insurance had never been renewed. The customer had then phoned up two weeks later to say they hadn't received their documents, only to be told that their insurance had never renewed.

104

This made me wonder: When they monitored the recordings of the calls, did they do it randomly, or did they pick and choose calls where they knew there'd been a consultant error that had been reported, like in this case, so the consultant would be more likely to fail? I'm not much of a conspiracy theorist, but this did seem like a good way for the company to save money by cutting our bonus for these mistakes.

Normally at lunch time, all of our team sat together in what they called The Assembly Room. Today though, everyone seemed to have different dinner hours so it was just me and Samantha sat there, eating our sandwiches. I mentioned that my pet rat had died the previous weekend and that I'd buried her in the garden. To explain what had happened to my young daughter, my sister had said that Minky the rat had gone to heaven. I didn't question it at the time but later, when my daughter was in bed, I brought it up. I'd thought it was strange to say she'd gone to heaven when neither my sister nor I believe in God, Heaven or religion of any sort. I'm not saying that God doesn't exist, just that he'd not been made evident to me and I didn't feel I had a need for religion in my life.

As I told Samantha this story she asked the next logical question: Was I doing anything special for Easter that weekend? I told her I had an Easter Egg hunt planned with my daughter, but other than that I was just hoping to have a chilled out day. She then asked me if Easter Sunday was the day we celebrate Jesus' death or rebirth so I told her it was to celebrate his resurrection. This is how it went:

Samantha: So did he die on Good Friday and got born again on the Sunday?

Phone Monkey: I think so, yeah. Didn't they teach you all the Jesus stuff at school?

Samantha: Oh, I never went to any history lessons, I was always hiding up on the school field, smoking with my friends.

Phone Monkey: History lessons? I think you mean RE. Religious Education.

Sam: No, I went to RE lessons, but they never mentioned Jesus there.

At that point I went into the toilets and started banging my head against the wall until my skull caved in.

It's A Strange World

Day Three Hundred and Seventy-One

My computer was unexpectedly slow to load today, so as 9am approached I had panicked a little. We had to be on the phone, ready to take calls dead on 9am or we got a stern telling-off from our manager. Occasionally our computers didn't load in time, and we had to ask a manager if it was okay to have some off-the-phone time until we were ready to start taking calls.

However, yesterday we were told that our entire floor had been underperforming and, as a result, all off-the-phone time had been banned. So I was informed today, much to my dismay, that I had to go on the phone and take calls, knowing full well that I would be unable to deal with any of the customers' enquiries. Basically I would have to answer the phone, take the customer's phone number and tell them I'd call them back in an hour.

What they didn't take into consideration though, were days like today when the entire floor's systems went down, meaning that not a single person could access anyone's insurance policies, and all we were actually doing was taking down phone numbers for callbacks, for four hours.

When I came back from dinner, the systems were back up again and we could start calling the customers back. But imagine this: I could take down a phone number from a customer in about thirty seconds. I was taking numbers for four hours so I had well over three hundred people to call back, and three hours in which to do it before my shift ended. The problem was immediately obvious. Even if every callback only took an average of five minutes, it would have taken me 25 hours to call them all back. Despite the futility of the task we all started doing our callbacks, in the order they called. At a rough estimate, I'd say that ninety percent of the people I called back had grown tired of waiting to be called back, had called us back themselves, and had their problem dealt with in another call centre. The other ten percent of people we had the chance to call were unhappy that it had taken us so long to call back. And approximately 250 customers were never called back. And this was not just how *my* working day went. Every person on my floor, and we numbered in the hundreds, were all forced to do this exact same thing, to the disgruntlement of tens of thousands of customers. And the managers thought this was a good and productive way to run a business which had previously maintained a relatively good reputation for customer service.

When I started my life as a Phone Monkey, 370 days ago, one of the first things we learnt about was the speed with which they wanted us to handle calls. Under no circumstances were we to try to build rapport with customers, and I frequently witnessed Phone Monkeys getting tied to a chair and being pistol-whipped for daring to break this rule. This hadn't bothered me at all; I was there to do a job and I couldn't have cared less about the customer's private life. Don't read that wrongly; I didn't think I was better than any of the customers or anything like that. It's just that I didn't see any reason for me to know everything about their lives. My job was to establish their needs regarding insurance matters and then sell sell sell.

Today we gathered around in the meeting area, to be told that as of today, that rule had been completely overturned. From now on we were going to get into trouble if we DIDN'T try to get to know each customer a little better. We were expected to utilise any sounds we heard in the background on the phone call to try and drag information out about the customer's life. If I heard a TV, I was supposed to ask what they had been watching, and tell them that I wished I was at home watching TV myself. If I heard a baby crying, I had to mention someone that I knew who'd recently had a baby and say how great I thought babies were. If I heard someone having a domestic I had to tell them that I regularly went home and beat my fictional wife with a stick. I think that's how this all worked. It made me wonder what went round in a manager's head when they felt we needed these drastic changes. I could kind of see where they were coming from. If I befriended a customer they were probably more likely to be easily led into buying one of our additional products. But things like just renewing someone's policy or sending out proof of no claims bonus just didn't require that level of intimacy. I bet they'd seen a statistic somewhere that said knowing your customers better increased profits by 12%, or something similar. I guarantee that this time next year they'll have turned it back around again when they realise that us talking to the customers for longer means that they had to hire more staff to process all the calls, and that extra profit they earned would be swallowed up by the new staff's salaries. If I could see this coming, why couldn't they when they were supposed to be the experts?

Hello?

Hello, you're speaking to Phone Monkey, can I take your policy number please?

Hello?

Is anyone there? Hello?

Can you hear me?

Tell you what, I'm not allowed to hang up a call without a really good reason so I'm going to sing a happy little song and you can feel free to join in on the choruses.

Hello?

Okay, here goes then...

Hello?

Oh, there you are. Don't worry, I've only been sat here waiting for you for three and a half minutes.

I wouldn't normally be so angry about waiting to talk to someone but let's remember the facts here: YOU CALLED ME!!!

I'm sure that whatever you decided to do between dialling this number and actually speaking to me was really important, but I don't get paid a great deal and all I really have left is my dignity, which you're stripping me of by making me wait. Tell you what, why don't you just sit there in silence again and I'll give you a back massage too?

Errr... I'll call back.

Don't bother.

Day Three Hundred and Seventy-Two

Today I'm going to talk to you about SPUD. Don't worry, I've not gone mad and started discussing potatoes, it's an acronym for Strategic Planning, Underwriting and Development. It's a team of people who regularly came into the business, looked at how we were doing things, and got us to strip away any extraneous information from our call guides. They also got to decide what we were allowed to have out on our desks (no personal items, no family photos, no mobile phones), and their work was supposed to make the business run more efficiently. They came into the business every six months or so, decided that at least half of the script we read on calls was unnecessary, stripped those sections out of the call guide and left. Then, one day at a time, our managers poked their nosey noses in, and started adding things back into the call guide, so by the next time SPUD poked their heads round the door, they would have to tackle the call guides again. It's a bit bizarre really, that our business would pay for these people to come in and do their job, when management effectively reverse everything they put in motion.

Ken was telling me today that he remembers the very first time SPUD came into the business:

"They were the good old days when you could come into work, have breaks at whatever time you wanted, leave a bit early as long as you made up the time on your dinner hour or the next day, and everyone was really friendly and easy to get along with, even management. Back then we had no call guide at all so it became very easy for us to sell things like breakdown cover on your motor insurance because we could do something called fear selling.

"What that means is that we could say things like, "I see your motor insurance policy has already lapsed. If you don't get your policy renewed right away, I'll have to inform the police because it's illegal to be driving without insurance," as a way to get them to renew there and then, for fear of incarceration. This went on for years and I've heard some fantastic stories of things people have said to customers to try to get a sale.

"One woman, Janice, was so intent on getting a sale that when speaking to the father of an 18-year-old policyholder, she said to him, "Are you sure you don't want breakdown cover on your policy? If your daughter was to be driving down a dark country lane and her car broke down, she'd be stuck there all on her own. And there's all sorts of dangerous people out on our streets these days. Killers, rapists... is that a chance you really want to be taking with your 18-year-old daughter?" And rest assured, he bought the breakdown cover.

"Another consultant, again asking about breakdown cover, wondered what the customer would do if he was driving out in the country and a cow wandered into the road, the car hit it and the cow exploded all over the front of the car, its intestines jamming up the inner workings of the car, and its blood painting the car red... Wouldn't you need breakdown cover in that situation?

"The things people used to say were verging on the ridiculous, but we always did it with tongue firmly in cheek. Then the SPUD team came in and decided that we were being too reckless, and that we needed to follow a strict set of guidelines, which over time evolved into the script we use today. They told us we had to start and finish our shifts when we were told, and only have breaks at certain times. They just came in and stripped all the fun out of the business. I know there has to be a certain amount of control and organisation, but what it's developed into today... It's like we have a million rules and regulations, and it's impossible for you to get through a month without being in breach of one of their terms and conditions. It used to be fun working here. Now I'm just waiting for my retirement so I can escape."

One of the main regulations the SPUD team had put in place was the Data Protection aspect of things. It was there to prevent us from making changes on the wrong policy, and to prevent people making changes to customers' policies maliciously. No one lost with Data Protection. I genuinely believed it was a good thing to have, but today I got into a lot of trouble when a customer refused to play by the rules. The call went like this:

Phone Monkey: Hi, can I take your full name and the first line of your address?

Customer: Yeah, it's Jack Martin, 23 St James's Park.

Phone Monkey: Thank you. And how many bedrooms are in the house?

Customer: I don't know.

Phone Monkey: You don't know?

Customer: No.

Phone Monkey: Oh, okay. What type of property is it then? Terraced, Detached, Bungalow?

Customer: I don't know. It's just a house. I've given you my policy number, can I make some changes to the policy now?

Phone Monkey: You just need to pass Data Protection, sir. How many bedrooms are in the house?

Customer: I've told you, I don't know!

Phone Monkey: If you can't tell me how many bedrooms are in the house or what type of house it is then I can't help you.

Customer: Get me your manager.

After speaking to the customer for two or three minutes, my Team Leader, Michelle, asked the customer how he normally pays for his policy, then transferred his call through to another consultant and told him to make the changes the customer had asked for. Michelle dragged me into an office and started laying into me.

"You were being purposely obstructive to that customer, and you told him that if he didn't give you the number of bedrooms or type of house then you couldn't discuss his policy. There's lots of other questions you could have asked; How he pays, what optional extras he has on the policy, any joint policyholder's names… and you didn't. It's not the first time you've been rude to customers and I'm going to have to write it up in a report and refer this to HR now, and let them decide what to do with you."

And all this because some idiot either wouldn't tell me details of his house, or he wasn't who he said he was and really didn't know the details. Either way, because of Data Protection laws, we shouldn't have made any changes to the policy as this caller requested. Yes, she's right, the customer is supposed to fail three Data Protection questions before we refuse to speak to them, not just the two that I stopped asking questions after, but come on… Who among you doesn't know how many bedrooms are in your house? And now my job was at risk as I now faced a Human Resources disciplinary. Wonderful.

The Test

Day Three Hundred and Seventy-Three

We all arrived at work today to find an envelope on each of our desks, containing our new hours which would commence in four weeks' time. We all knew there had been a change coming, and I had even chosen the Late Shift, but only because I thought there'd be no way they'd actually have us working until 10pm. My team was being split up into a number of different teams, and my shift was changing from 9-5 to 2-10pm. I'd be working until 10pm every weekday night. Some people on my team got slightly different shifts, but most of us got this ridiculously late shift, and I was surprised to see usually placid, quiet people slam their envelopes down on their desks and storm off. Carly and Michael from my team left the building and never came back.

Apparently people were walking out of every team in the building, and management started to panic that they might not have enough people to answer the phones so they decided to have an emergency meeting with all of us.

"First of all, we appreciate you taking the time to come to this meeting..."

(As if we had a choice.)

"...and let me tell you it's been a very difficult decision to extend the office hours to 10 o'clock at night, but it's a decision which will benefit the business and, therefore, yourselves."

(It didn't actually benefit us Phone Monkeys in any way.)

"A few of you have approached us about the bonus situation, and we're currently looking into ways in which you could increase your bonus; for example, selling one more Travel policy a day would earn you £10 extra per month. Selling one more Pet Insurance policy a day would add £15 to your month-end bonus."

(So we were expected to increase productivity basically, and we'd still only be on a fraction of what we were earning before. Fantastic.)

"Furthermore, I'd like to extend my gratitude to you all for making this company what it is today. We know we couldn't have got to the point where another company would buy us out, without your hard work and determination."

(Which you're rewarding with a pay cut.)

"All the managers will be walking the floor today, listening to your feedback and trying to offer solutions to any problems and ideas you may have."

(Listening with their ears stapled shut.)

In the space of one day, the company had managed to lose over a hundred members of staff who, through family commitments and other reasons, could not work the ridiculously late hours. The last bus from work left at 9.20pm so I wasn't exactly sure how they planned for the non-drivers to get home after their late shifts.

I still hadn't heard when my disciplinary was going to be, after the Data Protection debacle yesterday, but I was slightly worried about the security of my job, as without my income I'd be up a certain brown creek without a paddle!

Another way we tried to take our mind off the boredom and strictness of the job was The Squeal Factor. What we did was wait until someone was taking a call from a customer, then employed one of a number of distraction techniques. Sometimes we rolled up bits of paper and flicked them at the face of the Phone Monkey on the call, and sometimes we utilised various McDonald's toys which tended to be lying around the office, and make noises, right into the headset of the consultant so the customer could hear the noise too. Other times we just jumped out on each other, and the aim was always to get the consultant to squeal down the phone to the customer, and then have to explain themselves. Not surprisingly, we often got told off for this, especially in the evening when there were dozens of pieces of balled-up paper around the office, all over the floor.

There'd been a number of occasions when I'd finished work and been so stressed out that I'd wanted to go out for a drink with my friends. I think if your job makes you feel like this then you should probably be looking for a new job. The worst part of this was the hangover the following day. When any calls came through that weren't a standard renewal, the trick was to pass every other call through to customer services. This made your day a lot easier as only about 10% of our calls were renewals. Given all the options on the automated phone line when they rang up, customers always picked the wrong option.

Things We Wish We Could Say

Day Three Hundred and Seventy-Four

I missed my first four calls today, I signed onto my phone at the right time, then sat there chatting with other people on my team. Ten minutes into my shift I found it strange that everyone else had been taking calls, and I was yet to receive my first one. I checked my phone to make sure it was functioning properly. It said a call had just come through, a travel insurance renewal, but I could hear nothing in my headset. Then I realised I'd forgotten to plug it into my phone. By the time I'd plugged it in the call had gone. The customers had been getting through to me, hearing silence, then hanging up. Part of me wished I could leave my headset unplugged and sit there all day, watching the calls come and go.

My Team Leader, Michelle, pulled me into an office today, to discuss my disciplinary. She started off by saying how disappointed she was that she was going to have to refer me to HR, and ran through the details again, of what I'd said on the call. I admitted that I perhaps could have asked more questions to ascertain the caller's identity, but he was also in the wrong for not answering my very basic questions and being obstroculous.

But I had an ace up my sleeve. I'd been preparing for this meeting with my Team Leader before she passed her concerns on to the HR Department, and here's how the discussion went:

Michelle: So I've written out what's happened, how you were obstructive to the customer, and didn't ask as many Data Protection questions as you should have.

Phone Monkey: Yep, I agree. I should have asked more questions. I disagree slightly though, as it was him being obstructive.

Michelle: Well, it's your job to ensure customer satisfaction, even if it means biting your tongue sometimes.

Phone Monkey: Just to remind you, I've never failed a monitor for Data Protection before.

Michelle: What do you mean?

Phone Monkey: Well, whenever they listen to my calls, they never have a problem with the way I do Data Protection, and I feel I was doing my job in a manner which befits the importance of Data Protection and ensuring that we're talking to the right people.

Michelle: I'm afraid HR won't see it that way.

Phone Monkey: And what would HR do if they knew a Team Leader had spoken to a customer about specific private and personal details of their policy without them correctly passing Data Protection?

Michelle: Well obviously that would be a very serious matter. Why?

Phone Monkey: No reason. It's just that once you took over the call from me and spoke to the customer, you asked him one Data Protection question, about how he pays for his policy. However, our Data Protection guidelines state that if a customer fails a Data Protection question they then have to answer two questions correctly for each one they got wrong, so we can be sure we're talking to the right person.

Michelle: And?

Phone Monkey: And he failed two questions with me, then you only asked him one further question: How he pays. You then transferred him to another consultant to continue the call, after telling her she was okay to discuss the policy with him as he'd passed Data Protection. He hadn't, and if HR were to find out about that, they could easily listen back to the calls and confirm that what I'm saying is true. That could get you into a lot of trouble. It's not only against the rules: It's against the law.

Michelle: Why would you do that though?

Phone Monkey: Why would you report me to HR for doing my job and trying to ensure I was talking to the correct customer and not someone pretending to be him?

Michelle: I...

I had her. I wasn't 100% sure my ploy would have worked, but it did.

Michelle: Let's just forget about this then.

She tore the report up in front of my eyes. Disaster averted! And I now had something over my Team Leader that assured me an easy ride from here on in.

It couldn't have come at a better time really, because at the moment everyone was doing terribly on calls, and the customers were fleeing like we had the plague or something. Apparently the very first thing the new owners had put into place was a new pricing plan. Most policies had seen an increase of around £200 for the year. They knew this would make customers leave, but they were only doing it on policies they'd decided they didn't want to cover any longer. If you'd made a claim in the last five years, you were one of these people with the skyrocketing price. They only wanted people on the books who didn't make claims. Their manifesto said that they were happy to take our million customers and discard 800,000 of them, as long as we kept the 200,000 that were bringing pure profit into the business.

We Phone Monkeys were targeted on the percentage of customers we managed to retain though, and it was virtually impossible to save a customer when they could inevitably find the same insurance hundreds of pounds cheaper elsewhere. So our managers raised the price to purposely lose customers, then us Phone Monkeys got disciplined for those customers leaving. It made no sense at all, and the time we were taken off the phone to attend those disciplinaries for not hitting targets would have been better spent with us on the phone, trying to save the last few customers before every last one of them deserted us. The morale of this place had sunk like a stone in the last few days since the takeover, and I could only presume things would get worse when we all saw our payslips at the end of the month, with our reduced bonus on them.

*   *   *   *   *

I originally wrote a much shorter version of this Phone Monkey book, and had it for sale as a digital download-only book. Over a short period of time I sold over 40,000 copies of it, prompting my decision to take it off those book websites for a short time, until I could edit it into something which I thought was better, and get it published as an actual book (which is now in your hands). What always amused me about these book websites were the reviews I found. There were a surprising number of reviews left by people who probably shouldn't be allowed to have access to a computer, or anything electrical, really, in case they accidentally injured themselves. This was one of the reviews I received, and it was accompanied by just one star out of five:

"I did not receive this book and do not remember even looking at it, and I certainly never received it."

Rest assured, I had clicked "No", that review had not been helpful to me.

Invalidation

Day Three Hundred and Seventy-Five

Amidst all the hatred we had for management, very, very rarely they did offer a glimmer of hope for us Phone Monkeys, when a new job was advertised on our office notice board. The jobs were usually for Team Leader posts, as one of our current Team Leaders realised they could get a much bigger pay packet Team Leadering somewhere else, and left a vacancy. On occasions like that, dozens of Phone Monkeys applied for one post, and usually the most hated person in the office got the job, and we would spend months bitching about which of the applicants would have been far better suited to the role.

Today, however, the new job situation was different. Our company didn't only sell insurance. A branch of it, based in another call centre, also did debt recovery. When I first read the job sheet, I thought they were looking for people to go door-to-door, old-school style, smashing people's faces in and taking their possessions to be auctioned off to pay their debts. Sadly it wasn't anything as exciting as that, not that I would have been any good at such a job, being a bit scrawny as I was. It was just a case of us calling customers to try to convince them to set up a monthly payment plan to sort out their debts. It didn't sound any better or any worse than the job I was currently doing, but everyone needed a change sometimes, and having worked there for a year already, I was absolutely sick of the office politics and the ridiculous rules and regulations. I decided to apply for one of the jobs. The best part was, they were looking to expand the office which is most local to us, by fifty people, so the odds of getting a job there were definitely stacked in my favour. The fact that the job would revert my working hours back to 9-5 was another bonus, and there had been quite a buzz going round the office as we all dreamt of leaving for pastures new.

Ken came up to me at break-time today and told me he was halfway through reading the first section of my book on his Kindle and that he was really enjoying it. I'd made a point of not telling anyone at work that I'd even written the book because I didn't want my managers to find out and sack me, so I didn't know how he found out about it. The book was on Amazon as being written by Anonymous, but when I first listed it on there I put my own name on it as the author, and it sold 3000 copies before I thought better of it and changed it. I knew this was going to catch up with me at some point.

Something that always made me smile was when customers acted all polite when you were talking to them, then when the call was over and they hung up, sometimes they didn't hang up the phone properly on their end. I'd heard all manner of strange things. More often than not it was things like, "That ****ing idiot wouldn't knock my price down so I put him in his place," when all he'd actually done was politely request that we don't renew his home insurance. I'd also heard people screaming at each other about their dinner not being ready, and once I even heard someone say, "It's okay, he believed I was the policyholder," which meant that I had to refer the policy to our fraud department and the police will have been brought in to investigate.

Others, mostly elderly women, have said, "Awww, you should have heard him, he was such a sweet boy. He did me a special deal and got the price down for me." Again, all I did was my job, and offered a minor discount, but hearing them say that gave me an enormous feeling of self-worth, that I could make someone so happy with such a simple act, given how robotic my job had become.

There were lots of things that you learnt whilst working at an insurance company, that you wished you could tell every customer on every call. You all know that if you make a fault claim on your policy, your price will go up the following year. What a lot of you aren't aware of is this: You're one of those good drivers who doesn't claim, and has a relatively low insurance premium. However, when you make no claims for ten years, an alert is raised on your policy. The insurance companies expect that every driver will be involved in an accident at some point, and the fact that for ten, fifteen, twenty years you haven't made a claim means that each year you get one year closer to the likelihood of making your first claim. For this reason, they up your price each year after your ninth year of No Claims Bonus has been earned. The price will continue to go up each year after your tenth year until you make a claim when, unfortunately, they will put your price up even further. I had no idea how this could be legal or, if it is legal, how the managers involved could sleep at night, knowing how badly they were robbing the millions of people who insured their cars in this country and didn't ever claim. All I can say is this: Walking is free, people!

Day Three Hundred and Seventy-Six

To ensure that we were all doing our jobs properly, every few days our Team Leaders would call back a few of our customers to quiz them about the service they'd received from us. This was all well and good, providing that the customer selection process was fair. If they randomly picked three customers out of our working day (we had to log every single call we received so that would be an easy task), then they'd get an accurate impression of the quality of work we did. If this were the case, they'd find out that I was an impatient, rude and lazy Phone Monkey. However, this wasn't how they selected which customers to call back. They just asked us to pick out two customers ourselves and write down their policy numbers and what we sold or attempted to sell them. It was just a simple case of being nice to two customers a day, and writing those numbers down. As far as management were concerned, all of us Phone Monkeys were perfect little angels.

I'd had four other people at work come up to me in the last few days and tell me that they'd liked the first installment of my book, and that I was brave for daring to put my name to something so scathing of our bosses (they must have bought it before I Anonymized it). It seemed a lot of people knew about this book now, and I was becoming increasingly concerned. I had kids at home who were always asking me to buy them cool stuff, so the idea of being sacked was a very scary prospect since we relied entirely on my income. Everyone I'd spoken to had promised that they wouldn't tell anyone about the book or who wrote it, but word was spreading very quickly now, and when a team leader told me they wanted to have a word or ask me something, I was certain that each time would be the last time I had a conversation with anyone in the company.

Today was time for my Annual Performance Review. I couldn't care less about those things. We'd been told that no one was getting a pay rise that year anyway, since the new company wanted to make sure that we were worth the wages they were currently paying us before they decided to pay us more. I didn't know why they called it the Annual Performance Review since we had one every three months. They rated us out of ten, and this year I got a two. They based it on how many customers I'd saved versus their impossible targets, how long I took on each call, and things like how much overtime I did which, frankly, was none these days. When I first started and was full of enthusiasm, I would have been disappointed with anything less than ten out of ten. How times changed now that the company had been taken over. In this Performance Review it was made clear to me that I was not putting enough effort in. I didn't try to sell the customers life insurance when they rang about their home insurance, and I never offered them breakdown cover on their motor insurance.

You know when you've been in a job so long that it grinds you down, and you get up in the morning, finding yourself short of breath with mini panic attacks because you've got to go back to the monotony again? I had that virtually every day now. They'd become so strict on our targets to the point where I was not hitting any of our 21 targets (yes, twenty-one!), and we couldn't even go for a wee without first asking a manager's permission, which I was sure contravened some sort of human rights law. So I could have been doing better at work, yadda yadda yadda. My eyes glazed over and I started thinking about how many managers I wanted to throw from the roof, and how if I won the Euromillions I'd buy this entire company and sack everyone above Phone Monkey level. Yeah, yeah, two out of ten. So what?

It felt an awful lot like at any minute they could push the workforce slightly too far and everyone would leave the building, setting fire to the carpets on the way out so we could watch it all burn, satisfied that, in the end, we didn't let the bastards win.

What I couldn't deny was how much my life had improved as a result of getting this job. In just one year I'd earnt more as a Phone Monkey than I ever did in three years of being self employed, and for that I was very grateful. I'd worked my nuts off to earn that money though. I started off doing a lot of overtime, and generally doing whatever I could to earn as much money as was humanly possible, and it paid off when I was the recipient of an award for being the best salesperson in our building, which I think is quite an accolade given that there's over 500 of us here. It was just that when they started grinding you down with the rules and regulations that you found yourself wondering if it was worth all the bother. Why should I help this company out when they kept changing their rules so they could catch us out on one thing, or if I got that right, they'd bend a rule to mean that I'd not met a particular target. It's sad that they felt they had to treat the staff this way, and an employer with an ounce more sense would have looked at the situation and deduced that giving us slightly more bonus, or more flexible working hours would have made us produce the results they wanted, and better, without them always holding the threat of our future unemployment over our heads.

*   *   *   *   *

One place I worked for that had good management, was a cinema that I worked in for about a year whilst at university, and sadly, the cinema closed down and we all lost our jobs because of the remote location of the place. I say "all lost our jobs"; there was actually only a total staff of six, a sad representation of how quiet the cinema had become. I'd just completed my degree and was moving back home anyway, but it was still sad as the old cinema had become like a second home to me. The manager, a kind old lady called Barbara had given us the sad news about the closure but this cloud had a silver lining:

"I know we're closing and you're all going to have to find new jobs and it's very sad. Some of you have worked here for ten years and it's horrible that we have to close down. The bigger cinemas in town are newer and more flash, and we just can't compete any more.

"I was digging around in the basement over the weekend and I've found hundreds of old film banners, magazines, toys, and all sorts of cinema merchandise from the last few years. When this place closes they're demolishing the building, so anything you find down there, you can have."

We all rushed downstairs to see what this treasure trove held, and we were pleasantly surprised. These were the days when eBay was just getting started, and while the others only wanted a handful of things for their own personal use – a banner or two – I arranged for one of my friends to pick me up from work that night, and I cleaned out the room and filled the car. I had dozens of film banners, from Spider-Man to the Star Wars prequels, and on top of that I had a huge box of 400 tiny radios from the Ben Affleck Daredevil movie, which at the time wasn't as universally hated as it is now. Then there were dozens of assorted toys and smaller posters. If the carpet hadn't been tacked down, I probably would have had that too.

I gor straight on eBay with it all; I sold all of the Daredevil radios in a few weeks. The banners (some of which went back decades and were very rare) made me a lot of money. That cinema closing down netted me half a year's wages in selling off all that merchandise.

About a year earlier, before the other cinemas in town had opened, we'd hosted the UK premiere of a Disney film. I'll not say which one because this next story might get me in trouble...

There were quite a few celebrities in attendance, from Coronation Street and Eastenders actors, to footballers and musicians. It was an exciting time and as we were halfway through ushering the special guests to their seats, I suddenly realised that they were all meant to have been given a programme thingy which had been printed especially for the premiere. By then it was too late to go back to the storeroom and fetch the books so I decided that we weren't going to give any of them out. So at the end of my shift I had 200 limited edition Disney books that no one else in the world had, and I shared them with the three other members of staff who were on shift that night. Let's just say we made a little bit of money on eBay with those, and no one was any the wiser...

Sick Day

I was going to call in sick today. I rang the reception of our building and asked to be put through to my Team Leader.

Then the phone was ringing for about ten minutes and I was getting frustrated with having to wait to talk to someone. Then I started thinking about my day off.

I really need a day's rest. I've got the flu and I ache all over. I've been vomiting and sneezing almost non-stop. Also I've been leaking from a place no man should ever have to leak from.

But I also knew that if I didn't go in, tomorrow I'd have to fill out a million forms, they'd want to see a doctor's note, and I'd have to go to a HR interview where they'd tell me that if I had one more day off, I'd lose my job.

In the end, I just decided it was easier to go to work. So here I am.

And don't forget we're always here listening. There will be NO days off work.

Day Three Hundred and Seventy-Seven

I handed in my CV and application form for the job at the Debt Recovery arm of our business, and apparently they were looking for a quick turnaround, and to get interviews done in the next 3 days, and have the successful applicants in the post in about a week's time. Every time I handed in my CV for a job application, I often wondered how in-depth they would go when researching how honest you had been with your job history. I think I'd probably had about 20 jobs, maybe more, since I was sixteen, and yet I only ever declared four of them. This obviously left big gaps in my employment history, so I just shuffled the start and end dates of these four jobs around, so it looked like I'd been continuously employed for 15 years. If I were to be honest, every employer would look at my CV and say, " He's spent one month here, two months there, then had four months off work altogether, then done a month here. Don't even give him an interview, he sounds like a right slacker." And they'd be right, with the exception of this job, which I'd now stuck at for over a year, tedious though it had become.

Today's shift had been a little shorter than expected. As I left the HR office and entered the call centre area, it felt eerily quiet. People were at their desks, ready to take calls, but something had changed. Everyone was looking at me with a sadness, or sympathy, or pity or something in their eyes. They knew something I didn't. This surely couldn't be good. Had I inadvertently sworn at a customer yesterday? Or not logged off my phone last night and left it answering calls when no one was there to take them? This was all very strange. I felt the hairs on the back of my neck prick up as my building's manager approached me, and asked me to join him in the conference room. I shuffled in and sat down nervously.

Manager: I suspect you know why I've brought you in here.

Phone Monkey: Actually, no.

Manager: Your book.

Phone Monkey: What book? I thought we were allowed to read at our desks.

Manager: Don't treat me like an idiot. We know you've written a book about working here.

Phone Monkey: I struggle to write a shopping list. I certainly haven't written any books.

Manager: I thought you might deny it. That's why I brought some evidence. I know that you've changed your name on Amazon so it says it's written by Anonymous now, but I have it downloaded on this phone here, from someone who bought it before you had the good sense to change your name.

Phone Monkey: Hmm.

Manager: Do you have anything to say for yourself?

Phone Monkey: Have you read it?

Manager: I've heard enough about it from your co-workers to know that I don't need to read it.

Phone Monkey: There's nothing in that book that isn't true, apart from that a few of the names have been changed.

Manager: I hear there's some breaches of the customer's right to privacy in it.

Phone Monkey: Not at all. Everything is done anonymously. I looked into it before I published the book. I've not broken any rules or done anything illegal. I don't even say where I work in the book. It could have been written about any call centre in the country.

Manager: You're not exactly giving me a list of reasons as to why I shouldn't sack you on the spot. Do I not even get an apology?

Phone Monkey: Well, you don't have grounds to sack me for a start. I've not broken any rules or directly slandered anyone in particular, not by their real name anyway. And I'm not sure what I should be apologizing for. I've done nothing wrong. I saw a gap in the market for a book about the training of a call centre worker, and ran with it. I have nothing to apologise about. In fact, I'm proud of my achievements. Without even needing to advertise it, I've sold thousands of copies in just a few months. Where you proceed from here is up to you, but I'm well aware that you can't legally sack me for what I've done.

Manager: Well until we decide what we CAN do with you, I'm putting you on suspension. Go home, take today and tomorrow off, and when you come in on Friday you'd better have an improved attitude, because you'll be in a Human Resources disciplinary meeting and your chances don't look good at the moment.

Phone Monkey: That's fine, I know my rights, and I also know a good solicitor if this company attempts to use any underhanded tactics. I'll see you on Friday.

As I left the office, my knees went all wobbly. For all my confidence and bravado in front of the manager, there were a number of facts here: I probably had broken company rules, and possibly a data protection rule or two, during the writing of the book. I didn't know if they could fire me or not, and I also didn't know any solicitors, should it all go pear-shaped on Friday. Still, I was off home now, for a day-and-a-half of relaxation before my final judgement.

I'd always been a little concerned that one day this book would turn around and bite me, and it turns out I was right, although I didn't take great pleasure in reminding myself of it now. This had all become very real suddenly, and the possibility of me losing my job worried me. I spoke to my friend George about it.

George: How are you supposed to live if you get sacked?

Phone Monkey: I don't think I will.

George: How can you sit back and be so nonchalant about it?!

Phone Monkey: That's the first time I've ever heard anyone use the word 'nonchalant' in a sentence.

George: This could be serious, though. You've got two hungry mouths to feed; how do you suppose you're gonna be able to do that with no income?

Phone Monkey: I know, I know. I don't mean to make light of it. You know what I'm like. But I really don't think they'll be able to do anything to me. Worst case scenario: If they fire me, I'll apply for another job. If my pig-headed determination to write this book lands me in financial difficulties, I'll take any job going. Shop work, cleaning, office work, whatever. You know my family is all that matters to me.

George: Just don't mess this up for them. The last thing you want is having to go back and live with your parents again.

And he was right, of course.

Pleasant Customer

Day Three Hundred and Seventy-Eight

Waking up this morning had been a strange feeling. It was a Thursday, yet I wasn't going to work! I knew my future as a Phone Monkey was under threat and the image of me lazing around the house in my pants all day might be one that makes you want to be sick in your own mouth, but I couldn't wait. But while I certainly wasn't the most motivated of people, I could see a PR opportunity when it slapped me in the face. I'd been suspended from my job for exercising my right to freedom of speech. I knew who'd be interested in that: Readers of the tabloids!

I got on the old laptop and Googled the news editor of every major newspaper in the UK, then set to finding all the editors of local newspapers with readerships of over 100,000 to send my story to. I made a dozen or so phone calls and sent about 120 emails, and suddenly the wheels of progress were in motion. The plight of the poor little worker, versus the corporate machine would hopefully make for an interesting story. Then it was just a case of waiting for email replies and telephone calls from the various media outlets.

I hadn't really banked on any of the newspapers being interested in my story, I'd just figured it was worth a shot, and it paid off big time. Of the 120 newspapers I emailed, over 50 agreed to run a story about me the following day, and those fine periodicals called to find a bit more background information on me. Within 6 hours of sending my first message I had telephone calls from two local TV stations who wanted to run stories on their 6pm shows. I decided to decline those because, while they may have given me a bit more exposure, it would also mean putting a face to my Anonymous name, and I'd rather keep my name a secret for now.

Questions answered, quotes given, and a huge grin on my face, I got comfy on the sofa where I proceeded to watch movies for the rest of the day. The only problem was that my mind was fully active and racing. Tomorrow was a big day for me. Not only could I lose my job and become a minor celebrity in the papers at the same time, I also had my Debt Recovery job interview to prepare for, if I would still be allowed to even apply for it. To be honest, I'd been so caught up in my book-writing that I'd not even given it a moment's thought. I was sure that I would have something resembling a right answer for anything they could throw at me, given all the job interviews I'd attended in the past.

Wrong Number

Day Three Hundred and Seventy-Nine

The big day. I went into my meeting with my manager and his HR representatives for them to deliver their final judgement on me. To be honest, in this current job climate, the prospect of losing my job was not one I relished. I'd looked for other jobs on and off while working here, but never managed to find anything that I could really be bothered applying for. That decision was possibly going to be taken out of my hands and I could be in the job centre queue by tomorrow morning. This was how it went.

Manager: First of all, we want you to know how unhappy we are with your decision to write negative things about our company. I've had phone calls from MY manager today about an article he's seen in his local paper, down south, and I've seen similar stories in the local paper, and I've heard it's in at least one of the tabloids as well. What we've taken on board, however, is the fact that you never mention this company by name, even in the newspaper articles I can see you've given your story to.

Phone Monkey: So my job is safe?

Manager: Not quite. We are well aware, as you pointed out the other day, that we can't fire you for what you've done. But we don't want you working here. The idea of how angry it makes me that you could be so negative about the work we do here, while doing that job yourself is crazy. If I were to never see you again I would be a very happy man. You have no idea what kind of s***storm you've stirred up here.

Phone Monkey: So what are we talking about here?

Manager: You've applied for the job in Debt Recovery, am I right?

Phone Monkey: Yes I have. I thought it was time for a change.

Manager: And we couldn't agree more. We've had a word with the team that's doing the interviews and let's just say that when you have your interview this afternoon, you'll be getting a very positive result. The managers above me wanted you gone but they know it's not that simple, so they've arranged this as a less painful alternative.

Phone Monkey: You're fixing the interview so I get one of the jobs?

Manager: Your words, not mine.

Phone Monkey: Well, that's a pleasant surprise. I definitely appreciate the underhandedness of it all.

Manager: So go out there, pack up your desk, go to your interview, and I hope our paths never have to cross again. Don't forget to hand your pass in at the end of the day, because I don't want you sneaking back in here under any circumstances.

I couldn't have asked for a better result, and to make the day that little bit more perfect, all the news articles running in newspapers up and down the country had generated a lot of interest in my book. I did my obsessive daily check of my sales figures, and in one day alone I had sold over 2000 copies of Phone Monkey Part One.

Here's one of the articles written about me in a national newspaper. Something I wasn't expecting was that some of the newspapers would use whatever journalistic tactics they could to deduce my secret identity, and a number of them printed my real name, even though I'd never given it in any correspondence. So my anonymity went out of the window, but as they say, all publicity is good publicity. The only thing that disappointed me was that they'd aged me by a year. I was only 31, not 32!

Call Centre Worker Facing Dismissal Over Comments Made In New Book

In a modern society where we're told we have freedom of speech, every now and then a story slips through to reveal quite the opposite. Call centre worker ▓▓▓▓▓▓▓▓ has been suspended from work, potentially facing the sack in the next few days, over comments made in his new book "Phone Monkey". Mr ▓▓▓▓, from Rusholme, Manchester, discussed the way in which his unscrupulous employer, a large and very well-known insurance company, conned thousands of customers out of money each year.

He replied with a simple defence, "All I've done is describe things the way they are. If they weren't misleading the customers into paying more than they should, I wouldn't have had anything to write about. My "Phone Monkey" book is a collection of anecdotes based on my experience of working in that place. I didn't even need to exaggerate anything. Sacking me would be a massive over-reaction on their part."

▓▓▓▓▓ is considering legal action if the threatened dismissal goes ahead, and he hopes he'll have the public to back him up. His book, available to download as a Kindle e-book on website Amazon.co.uk, sold over 2,500 copies in the week of its release, with sales steadily rising, and surely a publishing deal and more beckon for its 32-year-old author.

He has asked that we do not print the name of the company behind this insurance scandal, confident that by maintaining their anonymity he can stay on their good side and keep his job.

We'll keep you posted here how this story pans out, but given the public's interest in insurance company scandals, we presume this won't be the last we hear of Mr. ▓▓▓▓.

Below: The book in question, "Phone Monkey: The Secret Diary Of A Frustrated Call Centre Worker".

My nerves for the job interview had now completely gone and a wave of calm washed over me as I entered the room, knowing that I could do no wrong and the job was guaranteed to be mine. They still went through the pretence of asking me their typical questions: Give an example of when you've worked as part of a team, what do you feel you can bring to this role, etc., and I wasn't entirely sure how many of the judging panel knew that the decision had been taken out of their hands. I answered half-heartedly. I'd usually go into these interviews with long stories already planned out, since job interview questions are interchangeable in pretty much every job you apply for. I sailed through it in less than ten minutes. Most other candidates had been grilled for around an hour each. I came out of the interview grinning away to myself, and Elvis and Ken inquired as to how it had gone in there.

Phone Monkey: They were tough on me, there were a lot of difficult questions.

Elvis: Do you think you've got it though? I remember you were saying how excited you were about the interview.

Phone Monkey: I suppose I'll have to wait and see. I'm quietly confident though.

I didn't think it'd be wise to let anyone know how I'd managed to land the job, in case anyone complained and got the decision overturned. Having no pressure to perform well in the interview had put a new spring in my step, and while others waited on tenterhooks to see if they'd got their job, I was on Cloud 9, unnaturally buoyant. As the day progressed I saw from some of my workmates' Facebook statuses that they'd got the job and would be starting there on Monday, so I felt it was only right to take that opportunity to announce that I too had been a successful applicant and would be joining them in our new role as Debt Recovery Monkeys.

As it turned out, the managers were so impressed with the quality of a lot of the interviewees that they decided to take on 60 staff, not just the 50 they'd originally planned. I wouldn't have liked to be in the call centre on Monday morning when they were 60 staff down. The constant red light on our phone terminal might possibly turn purple, and then black, as the customers queued up to talk to a panic-stricken Monkey.

As I left the building one final time, I handed in my ID card and felt a twinge of sadness. Not for the job; I'd hated 90% of the work I'd done there. But the people I'd worked with in that call centre had been some of the most interesting, intelligent, thoughtful and open-minded people I'd ever met anywhere. There had been plenty of idiots too, but you can't escape them in life. I'd keep in touch with some of them, but it was always hard to say goodbye to people who I'd spent eight hours a day with for over 13 months. I was going to miss all those people, even the idiots. I wouldn't miss the managers, and I hoped one of those Watchdog-type programmes would eventually catch up with what really went on inside an insurance call centre, so we could all start getting charged a more reasonable price for our products. Until then, it was on to pastures new for me, and I could continue my life pattern of getting a new job every year until I retired!

BOOK THREE:
DEBT
RECOVERY
MONKEY

Day One

When I left the insurance call centre I had been in a dark place. I'd been beaten down by a job that had gone from amusing to stressful over the course of a year. Before all the hoo-hah about my book, I'd had numerous discussions with my friends about possibly going to the doctor's and seeing how I could go on long-term sick, just to avoid that hellhole until I got a new job. They all warned me not to do that, but that situation came to a head pretty quickly anyway after the publication of the first section of the Phone Monkey book became well-known throughout the company and I was ushered out of the door pretty quickly. Rest assured, the old me who was trapped in that dark place was gone, left behind with the old job, and the original me was back to unleash his sharp tongue on the world. There was still plenty of fight left in me!

My first day in the new job had involved me and eleven other newbies sitting in a room watching a short video about people who had borrowed £100 from a bank because they were a little short and it was the week before pay day. Those short term loans had extremely high interest on them though and, by the next pay day, they found that they owed £200 back. Only by that point they couldn't afford to pay anything back because that initial £100 had been spent on luxuries like alcohol and cigarettes and they'd never got around to paying their rent that month. By their third month they'd borrowed a little more and they were then £1000 in debt. Needless to say, by the end of year one they were over fifty trillion pounds in debt and people like me, in my new role as a Debt Recovery Monkey, had to convince them to stop spending their money on unnecessary luxuries and pay the bank some of their money back. That was the theory anyway.

All twelve of us in this section used to work together, in some capacity at the old place, the insurance company. We all knew each other's names and it was definitely not going to take long to fit in here because we were like old friends already. We all sat and discussed something we had all been told by the manager when we first walked in this morning:

"Basically you'll be phoning people up from a long list of debtors we have, telling them that you're not chasing them for money, then gently reminding them that they owe X amount of money and we'd like them to start making repayments, even if it's just £5 a month. I'll warn you now, a lot of people are going to shout at you for what they perceive to be harassment, and a lot of them will hang up the phone on you. You won't be the first person to phone them. Every single person on the list who hasn't made any payments in the last six months will be called on a weekly basis until the debt is fully recovered. I hope you're not averse to a little harsh language because in this job you're going to hear a lot of it."

We then got shown the call guide. It was definitely a lot less oppressive than the ten or so pages that we had been forced to recite verbatim to 100 customers a day at the insurance company but it still didn't leave a lot of room for improvisation. It went something like this:

"Good morning, this is Phone Monkey, I'm calling on behalf of Bank X to tell you about a special offer we have on today. We're aware of how difficult it can be to pay back loans and debts in the current financial climate, but we can help you through these hard times with a very simple payment plan. All we're asking you to pay back is X (usually 1% of the total debt) per month and pretty soon you'll be back on track with your payments."

The plan was to then barter with the customer until you could come to some kind of mutually beneficial agreement whereby they'd start paying money and we wouldn't have to send bailiffs round.

An hour from the end of the first day we went live on the phones. We had a team leader hovering around in case we ran into any difficulties. None of us were nervous about making the first calls; Given that we'd all worked in the other call centre for at least a year each we'd been taking around a hundred calls a day from customers who were irate. Just over a 12-month span this amounted to over 20,000 calls per consultant per year. We obviously went into the calls with our hopes too high and they were about to be dashed. This was my first call:

Phone Monkey: Good morning, this is—

Debtor: I saw the number. This is Bank X, isn't it?

Phone Monkey: Yes it is, I'm calling about a sp—

Debtor: A special offer, right? Ha! Here, Janice, listen to this idiot! They're still trying the old "We've got a special offer" trick like they're trying to offer us a bargain instead of robbing us blind!

Phone Monkey: I can assure you, no one is trying to rob you blind.

Debtor: Now listen here, you little idiot. I'm sick of your people calling us up. I'm unemployed. My wife spends all day looking after the kids. Do you really think we've got the money to start paying you people off?

Phone Monkey: All we're asking for is—

Debtor: Forget it, I'm not interested.

CLICK!

And sadly that was how it continued on my next eight calls. I looked around the office at my fellow new starters and beyond them to where people had been working here for years, and all I could see was a crowd of glum, grey faces. People who had slowly been beaten down by the anger and frustration of people who fell foul of a system whereby they had access to money without fully understanding the implications of how they were going to be able to pay it back. I didn't blame the banks; people were responsible for their own self-control, but the banks made it so easy to facilitate a loan, and now people were living in fear of that next phone call because it was always going to be someone wanting their money back.

I didn't feel anger towards the rude customers, the angry ones who called me names that I'm too polite print in this book, or even the ones who pretended there was a noise on the line and subsequently hung up on me. I felt pity for them and that first day had exhausted me. I didn't know what I'd expected when I applied for the job, but this certainly wasn't it.

I walked out of the building at the end of the first day at my new job, after seeing the sad faces of those who'd stuck that same job out for years on end, and vowed to never go back.

And I never did.

Limbo

That night at home I chatted on Facebook to some of my friends about what I'd experienced, and how I'd just walked out of my job. But I didn't rest on my laurels. The same night I applied for fifteen jobs which were not all suited to my skills or qualifications, but I knew there was a possibility that at least one of those places must want to take a chance on me. There were receptionist jobs in solicitors' firms, trainee nurse's assistant or something like that in a hospital, an assistant manager's job in Tesco, and one that caught my eye... a Claims Handler for an insurance firm... luckily not for the same company I'd just walked out of. I filled in the application form and crossed my fingers.

Less than twelve hours later, at 9am the following morning, my phone rang and it was the new insurance company. The admission interview had a maths test with trick questions where none of the multiple-choice answers were correct. Luckily maths is one of my strong subjects and I breezed through it. Then I had to write a reply letter to an imaginary unhappy customer. They were impressed with my work and after making me wait in their seating area for nearly an hour, they came out and told me they would give me a second interview there and then to save me going away and coming back. They must have been impressed that I spotted all the trick questions. They said most people just guessed one of the answers and got it wrong. I was to learn later that even people who didn't realize there were trick questions were offered similar jobs to mine which, on reflection, was a little disappointing.

In the second part of the interview they ran through why I thought I'd be suited to the job and times when I'd worked well as part of a team and all that nonsense. Then they looked through my CV to find out what I had done in each job I'd had, why I left those jobs, what I enjoyed doing in each job, etc. To this day, no one had ever found me out for my CV only containing a handful of the long list of jobs

I'd actually had. Rest assured, within a couple of days I had the phone call telling me that the job was mine.

*   *   *   *   *

In this gap between employers, my mum convinced me to sign up to her dentist's surgery, since I'd been complaining about cold food hurting my teeth for some time. I was hesitant to say the least, given that the last time I saw a dentist, 15 years ago no less, I'd had to have my teeth drilled to have fillings. They hadn't applied enough anaesthetic and I had felt them drilling into the nerves in my teeth. Since then I'd just been too frightened to go back. I couldn't let the pain in my mouth continue though, so I booked an appointment to see my new dentist, Miss Miel.

As soon as I walked into her office my fears drifted away and this beautiful French dentist certainly lived put my mind at ease. When she told me she was going to have to drill my teeth to put new fillings in I didn't flinch once. I just stared up into those beautiful brown eyes and thought that she could do whatever she wanted to me.

I'm not scared of going to the dentist any more. In fact, I think my tooth is hurting now. I may have to go back and see Miss Miel.

BOOK FOUR:
CLAIMS

Day One

I was going to write another book about my training, in much the same way I did in the original Phone Monkey book but sadly it was not to be. There were twenty of us starting this new job around the same time and everyone else had started four weeks before me for some reason, and had received full training. When I started they didn't have anyone to put with me individually to train me up so they just stuck me in a corner and got me to read through their company handbook. It was at this point, only a few hours into my first day that I realised that I was going to have to train myself in how to do this job. I was sat next to someone who was taking calls so while I was meant to be reading this whopping great book I kept sneaking a peek at what she was doing, picking up ideas as to what the various computer programmes looked like.

We were an outside claims handler for lots of different insurance companies. Basically not enough claims were made to each company so some insurance companies didn't like to set up a dedicated internal claims team to deal with them as they'd have consultants just sat waiting by the phone for hours on end, which would obviously affect their profit margins. We dealt with all the claims for them, and took a small amount of money for each claim we logged, whether it was successful or declined.

The new job didn't pay as well as the old job, and I'd seen my pay cut by about 10%. Also there was no bonus. If I didn't have money coming in from my Phone Monkey books, I'm not sure how I'd have been able to cope, to be honest. A further strain on my wallet was the fact that I now worked in the middle of town, where there was a cake and pie shop literally ten seconds from the front door of the office. I was going to need a cake fund because I had no willpower whatsoever.

Directly behind me in the office, Noisy Sarah shouted her way through calls, being rude to customers and generally just not being very helpful. She had no patience for their problems and no tolerance for their ill tempers when they didn't get what they wanted. I was sure I'd seen her hang up on customers, then tell our team leader that the line just "mysteriously went dead".

On a daily basis I'd be dealing mostly with home, wedding, motor and travel insurance claims, all of which I'd kind-of worked with before, albeit from a sales point of view. Something I learnt today which may interest is you is that travel insurance was originally designed just to cover you for medical expenses incurred in foreign countries. For example, in the US if you went to the Emergency Room, you would be billed not only by the hospital, but by every consultant you saw, whether that was just for a check-up, an x-ray, or an operation. Everyone charged. Bills for something like a broken arm being diagnosed and set in plaster could cost you upwards of $10,000. Living in a country where the NHS provides high-quality health care for free, I found this very strange, and I felt one of those rare moments of pride in being British.

Over time, travel insurance policies expanded, primarily so one company could sell more policies than another. One would add cover for lost baggage. Another would add cover for travel delay. Another for items stolen from your luggage. But the reality was that none of the other aspects of your travel insurance were really any good, apart from the medical cover. If you lost your £500 watch, the policies would all take deductions off for wear and tear, not to mention the fact that the most you could claim for was £100 per item. In most of the insurance policies I'd looked at today, there was a disclaimer at the back saying:

"While this policy does offer some cover for items lost or stolen abroad, we also recommend that you take out separate cover with your home insurance to ensure you're not left out of pocket when making property claims on your travel insurance."

So the policy itself even told you that it was not going to cover you and recommended that you look elsewhere!

The customers I'd heard today seemed a lot calmer than those I had dealt with when I was in the cancellation and sales departments of the other company. Even the angry ones were easily tamed, and it looked like I was going to enjoy this job.

The Exaggerator

Day Two

I started taking calls today, with someone listening in to me to make sure I was doing everything right. Everyone else that worked here had been here for over a month already so I should have felt a bit insecure about them all being better at their job than I was, but I was so used to dealing with customers on the phone that I just dove straight back in and didn't let it faze me. The computer system was so much more straight-forward than the one I had worked with at the old place, so it was really difficult to make any mistakes.

In between calls we dealt with the post that had come in that day, which was usually people's medical certificates, proof of their holiday booking, and loads of receipts for things that just wouldn't be covered by their insurance. Then the detective in me had to come out, piecing together all the pieces of the claim puzzle, so I could make a decision on whether or not we were going to pay the claim, or if we needed more information. It was nice to have the responsibility of this job, after working for over a year taking simple calls about the price of the insurance a million times a day with nothing else to offer any kind of relief in between the calls. I felt like I was actually using my brain for once, trying to decipher doctors' handwriting and figure out if people were trying to make fraudulent claims.

The downside to the new job was the walk to work, which was just under three miles. Every day I went to work I tried to take a slightly different route, desperate to find the quickest way because I absolutely hated the boredom of walking on my own for that sort of distance. I'd tried listening to music while I walked but I still got frustrated. I think at 31 years of age I should probably learn to drive. The problem with that being that I wouldn't trust other people's lives in my hands.

Every morning when I left the house I was inevitably running at least ten minutes late and I had to power walk. I was not a fit person. I was certainly not overweight or anything, but I got out of breath running up the stairs so I wasn't a fan of the power walk.

Every day when I got to work I found myself wondering how long it was going to take for my beer gut to waste away with all the walking. I'd had this bad boy since I was about 25 and it was showing no signs of disappearing yet. I'd join the gym but... well, you know me... it all seemed too much like hard work.

However, in my first positive step towards leading a healthy lifestyle, I gave up drinking 5 months ago. Given that I was in a gigging band where payment was usually in beer this had been a bit of a problem. My bandmates couldn't believe it at all. I'd gone from drinking ten pints every time we gigged (which was two to three nights a week) to drinking nothing but lemonade. I'm sure some people might tell you that the craving for alcohol eventually goes away but I'd found that it didn't. Every time I saw my friends drinking I was immensely jealous. I knew I had to be strong though, and I hadn't wavered once in my abstinence.

Let me go back a bit, because I don't feel like I'm being entirely honest with you here. I'd not only stopped drinking because I was thinking of my health, although that was one of the reasons.

The main problem with my drinking was the sleepwalking. I sleepwalked from time to time anyway, probably every couple of months or so, but it had got to the point that if I had two pints of beer or more, I was guaranteed to sleepwalk. Some people I'd explained this to had said that I just got so drunk that I didn't remember doing or saying things, but I certainly didn't get mind-meltingly drunk on only a couple of pints. One night I had wandered into my housemate's room and, whilst asleep, engaged him in conversation.

Phone Monkey: How do I hold the hamsters?

Housemate: What? What are you doing?

Phone Monkey: I need to know how to hold the hamsters!

Housemate: Just go back to bed, what are you going on about?

Phone Monkey: I don't want to hurt them, I need to know how to hold them!

I then apparently went downstairs for ten minutes, then came back upstairs and went back to bed. The next morning my housemate told me what I'd said and it was news to me. I ran to the cage where I kept two tiny Russian hamsters and luckily they were both fine. I didn't know if I had got them out that night but from the sounds of it I was definitely downstairs long enough to have had them both out.

Another time I woke my housemate up when I was moving a pile of clothes from in front of a cupboard door in my bedroom. He popped his head around the bedroom door to see what was going on.

Housemate: What are you doing in the dark?

Phone Monkey: I need to get in the cupboard.

Housemate: Why? It's the middle of the night!

Phone Monkey: I need to get some blackberries.

Housemate: What?

Phone Monkey: Oh, don't worry about it. I think there's some downstairs.

The next morning he told me that I'd gone downstairs and had been banging around in cupboards for half an hour, in the dark. I don't know if I ever found any blackberries.

At lunchtime today I ventured out of the office to look around some shops, and a few people I work with were sat outside the building in their cars, eating dinner. I didn't know why. There was a canteen in our building, there was a nice park two minutes walk from where we worked, or they could eat at their desk. Why would they be sat in their cars to eat? I just didn't understand some people.

We were a relatively new team so during the transition period they'd recruited someone from down south: Nigel, to help our team leader out with checking we were doing our jobs properly. He was about 50, overweight (his head appeared to have sunk into his shoulders, thus alleviating the need for him to possess a neck) but he seemed pleasant enough. If we asked him a simple question though, he turned it into a four-hour lecture about how he'd worked for loads of different big companies, and how fraud was a massive concern, and how he once had a claim that was for over £100,000. Christ, Nigel, I only wanted to know what time it was!

Something that concerned me a little was the high ratio of death calls. Claims where the policy holder had died, or someone they knew had died, or someone who was ill in hospital... with a terminal diagnosis. I had to tread very lightly, as I was not really known to be the most caring, considerate person around. Yes, I knew how it felt when someone you loved died, but my problem was that I didn't really know what to say when someone told me they'd just lost someone. We were told to acknowledge the death and get on with the business of processing their claim, but it was difficult and I'd found myself lost for words a couple of times. I suppose I would get used to it eventually, but this was an example of what happened, just when I was asking Data Protection questions on a call today:

Phone Monkey: Hi there, can I take the first line of your address?

Female customer: Yes, it's 36 Queen's Road.

Phone Monkey: And your telephone number?

Female customer: 555-607-8845.

Phone Monkey: And the reason for making your claim?

Female customer: My daughter died. My baby, it was a stillbirth. I had to cancel the holiday.

Phone Monkey: Oh, I—I'm sorry to—

Female customer: It was supposed to be our honeymoon. I gave birth to her on our wedding day but she was born dead.

Phone Monkey: I----------- um-----

There just aren't the words to express how she must have felt. I was a parent myself and I couldn't contemplate those emotions. I got tears in my eyes. She was crying on the phone. She was only claiming for a cancelled holiday and the loss of £200. I bet she'd rather have not claimed at all and waved goodbye to that money than have had to keep going through what happened to cause the holiday to be cancelled, especially because I had to ask for a death certificate to substantiate her claim. A death certificate for a baby. Rest assured, I didn't ask that question on Data Protection any more, I asked for their email address instead. Damn you, Data Protection questions!

*　　　*　　　*　　　*　　　*

When I was at university I decided that I wanted to be a TV writer. This was a strange realization because I'd never really excelled at writing and I famously didn't have many original ideas. But on I plodded, and before long I'd fully scripted a two-hour TV movie called Tax For The Stupid. It was about two lads winning the Lottery and falling out over the money they'd won. There's a similar programme on TV now, called Winners and Losers, but I wrote mine nearly a decade ago. I'd basically decided that people who bought Lottery tickets were idiots since the odds of winning were so remote (incidentally, I still buy Lottery tickets today), and that it was just a tax for stupid people. I probably shouldn't have submitted it to the BBC. I got a nice polite rejection letter saying it wasn't the sort of thing they were looking for. As a side note, I read somewhere that you're more likely to be killed going to buy a lottery ticket than you are to win the jackpot on that lottery. Food for thought, my friends.

I didn't let my BBC rejection put me off though, and got to work on my second script, a much more ambitious project. My plan was this: Launch a new reality TV show following two cops on their beat. The twist was that everything would be fully scripted and the two men in the show wouldn't be cops at all. Then when the public became interested in these cops' stories, in episode four one of the cops was going to get shot on a raid that the cameramen followed them around on, and he would be near death for a few episodes, before making a full recovery in the final episode. There'd be "live" scenes shot in hospital and hopefully the audience would sympathise with the injured cop and viewing figures would rise as the papers got wind of the sob story. Then I'd reveal that it was really all fiction and there'd be uproar. That was the plan anyway, although I never got round to finishing writing that one. I would probably have become the most hated man in TV for deceiving people, which I could probably do without.

Instead I started applying for jobs at Cosgrove Hall animation studio, who produced such hits as Count Duckula and Danger Mouse, purely for the reason that former Stone Roses guitarist John Squire, who I'd become obsessed with, used to work there. I never received a reply to my three portfolio submissions to them. Oh well, bigger and better things, and all that. Or at least that's how it was supposed to work!

166

Let's Be Friends

Day Three

In my last job I had felt powerless. I had just been a machine applying discounts and trying to get rid of the customer in three minutes or less. Here I had a reasonable level of power. I could make the decision as to whether or not your claim was going to be accepted. I could pay you thousands of pounds or I could pay you nothing and report you for potential fraud.

Today I started taking calls completely on my own, as management had decided that they couldn't afford to spare anyone to train me up any longer. They trusted me to fly solo, with no real training, on my third day of working there. I'm glad they had confidence in me, but I assure you their belief in my abilities was misplaced. Nonetheless I knuckled down and got on with my duties and I'd picked up quite a lot from listening in to calls for a few days and trying a few with supervision yesterday so I was okay. I find that all call centre work is just the same job but with an interchangeable script. At least they didn't seem to be as strict with the script aspect of things here and I could actually talk to customers as if they were human beings, rather than some strange robots who I had to talk to mechanically.

Sometimes I got really snotty customers who talked down to me and I liked to take the extra effort, when they were making a claim, to fully read them their insurance policy wording so I could point out to them exactly why they weren't covered. It became a challenge, trying to find loopholes and reasons why I didn't want to offer any cover to angry idiots. As long as I could find a sentence in the policy wording that suggested something similar to the customer's situation then I could get out of paying anything, and I took great pleasure in doing so.

It made me read all my own policy wordings, on my home insurance and travel insurance, just so I knew what I wasn't covered for,

168

because I knew how intricate the wordings were and it made it difficult to know when exactly you were going to be covered.

Something that customers kept saying was, "You're just trying to make up excuses not to pay my claim," and they were never satisfied by my explanation that it didn't matter to my company whether we had to pay the claim or not. We were not the insurer, we just dealt with claims on their behalf. I could have paid out £1000 or nothing, and it didn't affect how much our company got as we were paid by the claim, not by how many times we declined.

After sweating buckets in the office yesterday, I had decided to wear a thin, short-sleeved shirt to work today. And today they decided to turn the air con on full blast, and I swear there's a family of penguins building an igloo in the corner, content that our office is actually colder than their usual home.

Nigel started looking at some of our claims and letting us know whether he thought we were doing our jobs properly. He had no complaints about any of my claims so far but from what I heard, he didn't look into the claims in any great depth, and he was famous for missing things. He had told one girl she needed to find out how much someone's car repairs had been, when the estimate from the garage was quite clearly the first document attached to the file. I overheard him talking about Sarah from my team at dinnertime, saying that she was a pretty young girl. He wass 50. She was 23. Cue vomiting in my mouth. It didn't help that Sarah had decided today that instead of Nigel we should all start calling him Nizza. Oh dear. I just knew that at some point, someone was going to shout an accidental racial slur across the office when addressing him.

I was getting into the swing of things, processing a few claims, when there was a loud "BOOM!" from behind me. I nearly jumped out of my skin. The girl behind me had decided to shout "Boom" every time she declined a customer. She didn't say it to the customer obviously. She muted the call, shouted, "Boom! Decline!" then went back to the customer to apologise and say, "I'm very sorry sir, you're just not covered for that on your insurance."

Last weekend, before starting my new job, I went out for a drink with some friends who were leaving their jobs as Teaching Assistants to become fully-fledged teachers. This is how our conversation went:

Phone Monkey: What subjects do you teach?

Teacher 1: We all teach Social Sciences.

Teacher 2: For the kids who are naughty. The ones who disrupt classes and spoil it for everyone else.

Phone Monkey: I've got to admit, they didn't have Social Sciences when I was at school. What is it?

Teacher 1: It's teaching these kids social skills that they can use in the real world when they leave school. They're all academic under-achievers so we try to prepare them for life in other ways.

Phone Monkey: I remember you saying once that the kids you teach are all 14 or 15. What social skills can you teach them? Like saying "Please" and "Thank you" and how to do well at job interviews?

Teacher 2: No, we teach them things like crossing the road safely.

Phone Monkey: I know you're lying now.

Teacher 1 : No, we do! They need to learn these things!

Phone Monkey: I'm pretty sure I was crossing roads on my own when I was six years old. What else do you teach them?

Teacher 1: The other day we took them out ice skating, but the real lesson was getting on the bus safely.

Phone Monkey: And these kids are 15?

Teacher 2: We also teach them how to walk on the pavement and not stray onto the road.

This worried me. A generation of children who couldn't walk on pavements efficiently?

Day Four

Another of our everyday duties was Fraud Detection. An example of when I raised a concern was this:

Phone Monkey: Okay, can you describe for me the contents of the bag that was stolen from the coach?

Dodgy customer: Yeah, there was my iPad, some CDs and a cheap MP3 player.

Phone Monkey: Have you got the receipt for the iPad?

Dodgy customer: Yeah, it was £499, I only bought it three months ago.

Phone Monkey: No problem. So is that everything that was stolen?

Dodgy customer: I think so, yes.

Phone Monkey: Okay, I've got to let you know that as per the terms of this policy you're only covered up to £100 for what we class as 'valuables'... basically items that we consider to be highly likely to be stolen, like an iPad.

Dodgy customer: Only £100? Oh... hey, wait a minute, I think my wallet was in the bag too. Yeah. And I had £400 cash in there with the iPad. Can I claim for that as well?

With those types of customers we had to send a report to our fraud department who then called the customer themselves and asked lots of probing questions to try to trick the customer into telling two contradicting stories, in which circumstance they could then decline the claim outright for them attempting to defraud their insurance company. I didn't actually know what happened after that point. Did they get reported to the police? Did we send them nasty letters about what naughty little people they were? All I knew was that there was so much fraud going on in insurance in the UK that your total annual bill for all the insurances you have (Home, Motor, Travel, Pet) was around £180 higher than it would be if no one committed fraud. That's how big a problem it is.

There are a lot of people who thought, "I've paid £200 for this insurance, I'd best make a claim on it so I don't end up out of pocket." Insurance was not there to ensure that you were completely reimbursed for your losses, it was there to offer a cushion and help you recover as much of your loss as possible. Adding items to a claim that you never actually owned might have offset the cost of your insurance policy but it was illegal and we had our ways of finding you out so be very careful in the future!

Another clear sign that you were committing fraud was claiming for relatively high-value items (phones, computers, large quantities of cash) and not having any receipts. I knew from my own experiences that virtually no one kept their receipts these days, but we live in such a modern world that almost all large transactions were paid for on a bank card, because who just happened to be walking around with large sums of cash in their pocket? Banks now allowed you to trace your bank statements back for up to ten years, meaning you could prove you bought something with your bank statement. If you can't prove this, then the odds are you're making a fraudulent claim.

The problem is that 90% of people making claims exaggerated what had happened. If in doubt, we reported it as fraud. Report 'em all, let God sort 'em out.

Some people didn't intend to defraud their insurance, but they had interfering family members who thought they were offering good advice. I had this old lady ring me today:

Old lady: Hello, young man. My granddaughter has told me I should put in a claim for an injury I got on holiday.

Phone Monkey: Okay, did you incur some medical expenses while you were away?

Old lady: No, what it was is this: I went on holiday, on a cruise, and when I got back I got on the coach which brought me back to my house. When I stepped off the coach I walked across the pavement to my house, and tripped on a paving slab between the pavement and my garden path. I badly bruised my knee and had to go and see a doctor.

Phone Monkey: Right...

Old lady: And my granddaughter says I should be able to claim some sort of damages from you because the policy specifies that the cover only stops once you reach your home, and I was nearly home, only a few feet away, but the injury still occurred while I was technically on my holiday.

Phone Monkey: You're not covered for that.

Old lady: Are you sure? My granddaughter said I would definitely be covered for it. I even offered to give her a cut of any money I could make in the claim.

Phone Monkey: What you're describing right there is illegal.

Old lady: So I can't claim against my insurance?

Phone Monkey: No. We only cover for any out-of-pocket expenses so that's definitely not covered. It might be worth having a word with the council though, if the pavement outside your house isn't flat.

Old lady: Will they pay out?

Phone Monkey: You are exactly the reason that I hate the UK right now. This compensation culture will be the death of us all. Why don't we all just sue each other so much that we all end up with no money?

Okay, I might not have said the last sentence. She asked who to call at the council in relation to her uneven path. I said I had no idea.

I was flying solo again today and my team leader wasn't worried that I wasn't asking too many questions. I could have been making any number of mistakes on those calls and they weren't even asking me if everything was okay! So far today I'd paid out over £1,000,000 of claims. Okay, maybe not. But I'm sure I will one day. For now I'll settle For Mrs Williams' claim for £16.50 worth of socks that she left in the hotel by mistake.

Sarah, having heard that Nizza found her attractive, had started to play on it. I heard her asking him if he's single and demanding that he make her a cup of tea every day until the day he left. He was clearly smitten and did as she asked, providing tea whenever her booming voice demanded it. Please remember, he's twice her age and looks a bit like Jabba The Hutt.

I invented a new game today: The double boom decline. Basically the aim was to decline someone's insurance claim twice in one go. Not by declining somebody who's entitled to make a claim, but by spending as long as possible scouring the policy wording to find not one, but two, reasons not to pay out on a claim. An example of this is somebody who cancelled their holiday due to an illness but BOOM ONE they didn't do so on a doctor's advice, they just decided not to travel without consulting anyone. And BOOM TWO, the excess, or deductible, was higher than the cost of their holiday anyway, so even if they could claim, they'd get nothing. I'd heard rumours that someone in one of our other sites got a triple-BOOM-decline but I think it's just an Insurance Claims Urban Legend.

There was a bag of sweets regularly making its way round the office. People alternated in who was buying them but I refused to buy any, not because I'm tight or grumpy, but because I ate enough sweets at home, I didn't want to participate at work too. I was dreading the day when they would tell me it was my turn to provide them because then I'd have to have this discussion with someone and I'd either look like The Grinch or Billy No-Mates.

It was a much more relaxed atmosphere there than in my old job, but I'd noticed that some consultants were getting quite irate and rude with their customers. There wasn't the constant fear of one of your calls being listened to by a snooping snitch here though. I found myself a lot more at ease discussing things in great depth with the customers about their policies, and telling them what they were not covered for, even though I was still new and I didn't really know what I was talking about. I'd spoken to a lot of the consultants there who had never been pulled up on any mistakes they made on calls so I didn't think I'd have anything to worry about.

All The Essentials

Day Five

When I got into the office this morning I was asked if I could go on the phones five minutes before the start of my shift and take those five minutes off, later in the day. I found this very strange, particularly when I was told it was because they had three calls waiting. At the last place I worked, there would have regularly been over a hundred calls waiting. I obviously can't reveal the name of what that company was, but I knew for a fact that I would never take out an insurance policy with them because I knew what the queuing time was likely to be if I ever needed to call them. In my new job they panicked when there were three calls waiting. This was busy season. Three calls. I think this is going to be the best job I've ever had.

One of the few things that's been carried over from my old job is everyone's enjoyment of customers who had funny names. So far I'd dealt with a woman called Alice Cooper, and others on my teams have spoken to Mr Hermit, John Thomas and Mr Greedy. One lad who sat near me spoke to a customer and it didn't really go as planned:

Ryan The Phone Monkey: Hi there, can I take your name?

Customer: Yes, it's Mrs Haw.

Ryan: Is that spelt W-H-O-R-E?

Customer: No. H-A-W.

Ryan: I'm really sorry. I wasn't calling you a whore.

Customer: Get me your manager.

On the same day that Ryan took that call I spoke to Mr Fluffy for the first time. He didn't sound very fluffy. He should have been called Mr Shouty.

Customers presumed, as I would have too if I didn't work here, that when you called to make a claim you were talking to your insurance company. I was constantly having to explain to the customers that we were not their insurer, we didn't have any details about them whatsoever, we just logged the claims and asked them to send their documents in. I'd had so many arguments with customers that week who couldn't understand that until they picked up the phone and rang to make their claim, I had no idea who they were.

Sarah made a comment to Nizza that he'd not contributed to the sweet fund today and that he should buy the next bag of sweets at lunchtime. Like the dutiful little puppydog that he was, he went out and bought a bag of chocolates just for Sarah and said, "They're not for sharing, those ones are just for you."

She was understandably a bit freaked out by this man over twice her age doing this so she decided the best option was to share the sweets out with everyone. Towards the end of the day, Nizza realised what she'd done and confronted her about it, in front of a group of us. He told her off for sharing them with us when they were meant as a personal gift. I don't think he was aware of how much of a lecherous old man he came across as. I could smell a sexual harassment lawsuit on the horizon.

A man rang up to complain that our phone number wasn't free to call. He didn't want to make a claim, he rang us up just to say that. And it cost him to do so.

At thirty-one years of age I definitely didn't consider myself old, or even getting anywhere near approaching old age. I still played in bands and I liked new music as much as all the youngsters I worked with. Maybe calling them youngsters shows a bit of middle-agedness creeping in, but I was definitely cooler now than when I was 20 years old. When I met people now and they ask what I do for a living I could quite happily tell them that I'm the author of a successful self-published book for which I have zero expenditure, but that every month various e-publishing companies stuck a bunch of fivers in my bank account. This definitely put me in a different coolness league than telling people I answered phones for thirty-seven hours a week. Still, I wasn't technically lying so I didn't feel bad about it. Anyway, back to the kids at work... they'd started talking in a new language since I started working here. A typical conversation might go like this:

Phone Monkey: What was that claim about?

Sarah: This woman said she'd lost her iPhone but she was blaters deffo lying.

Phone Monkey: I don't know what you just said.

Some of them had even taken the very annoying step of not laughing at jokes told in the office. Instead they would smile and actually say "lol" or "rofl" (pronounced roffle) out loud as if they were part of some living, breathing text message. The latest trick was to say things like "just saying" or "what a psycho" but saying them in Twitterspeak, adding a hashtag prefix. "Hashtag just saying," was a regular phrase you might hear in our office.

And if I heard anyone say that anything was EPIC one more time I would quite happily have thrown my computer through the window and jumped to my death. What you just said was not epic. That photo is not epic. When you went out drinking IT WAS NOT EPIC. STOP SAYING EPIC!!!

When someone asked me if I wanted to join the Lottery syndicate, I heard a little voice in my head saying "I totes would," then I sighed at what they were turning me into.

My new workmates looked at me with pity when I told them that when I was at school we didn't even have the internet. I didn't get my first mobile phone until I was nearly 19 and I'd gone off to uni. I think my friends and I look back on our childhood days now and wish there had been mobile phones. I was notoriously late for everything. I even turned up late for job interviews and still managed to charm my way into jobs. When I was at school we used to arrange to meet up on a Saturday morning at 10am outside Woolworths, because that was the first shop you came to when you left the bus stop. I'd always turn up closer to 11am, and they'd all still be stood there waiting for me, looking particularly grumpy. This is something that modern teenagers don't have to put up with any more. They can just text each other and say, "I'm running a bit late, I'll catch up with you later on," although it would probably read more like, "Runng l8, c u l8r." Sigh.

I felt particularly young today though. I had to nip into town on my lunch break to get some money out of the cash machine. As I was walking away from it an old man approached me. I say old; he was only about 50. He asked me if I could show him how to use the ATM. I looked at him for a second because I thought he had to be joking. Cash machines have been around for as long as I can remember, which is probably something like 25 years. I know we use them much more now than we ever did, but I still found it strange that someone his age had never drawn money out of a hole in the wall. I went to show him how to do it and he asked if he could give me his card and pin number so I could just do it for him as he was scared the machine might swallow his card. Can you imagine if I'd been a slightly less honest person, and I'd just run off with his card and gone on a spending spree? I told him not to give me his pin number, and just showed him what to do, looking away as he entered his number. Out of the corner of my eye (could you have resisted looking?) I saw that his pin number was 1234. How had this man survived in the 21st century?!

Sensitivity

Day Six

On my way to work this morning I walked past a small wooded area as I usually do, but today I saw something out of the corner of my eye. I thought it was a dog. I turned to look, and about ten feet away from me was a rabbit. The biggest rabbit I've ever seen. It was as big as a German Shepherd dog. It looked me in the eye, stamped its back foot and ran off. I tried to keep up with it, jogging slightly along the path, so I could photograph it to show people. I just couldn't keep up! I don't know where this mutant rabbit came from but every time I walk past this area in the future I'm going to be very wary in case it jumps out of the bushes and tries to drag me off.

A sweet old man called up today and said he'd had to cancel his holiday, because his pet dog had a cold. I thought he was joking at first and laughed out loud. When he asked me what I was laughing at I had to rein it in and act all professional. I understood that people grew very attached to their pets but let me fill you in: If you cancelled your holiday because your pet was ill, you would not be covered by your travel insurance for a refund.

Something that annoyed me was when someone made a claim, then complained that they had to pay an excess. The way I saw it was that if you didn't have insurance you would get nothing if you had to cancel your trip for unforeseen circumstances. With insurance, as long as you got more than what you bought the insurance for, then you were winning. I'd seen people take out an insurance policy for as little as £1, then complain that we would only cover £500 worth of their £600 claim. Some people were just never happy.

*   *   *   *   *

I've always been on the lookout for ways to make money that didn't involve doing good, honest work, and when I was at university I used to write three or four letters a week to big food companies complaining about some aspect of their products to try to get some

184

freebies or food vouchers out of them. I made a good living doing this, and I'd say that at least half of the food I bought was paid for by these companies. My favourite of all the letters I sent was this:

"Dear Mr. Heinz,

I recently bought a can of your Pokemon pasta shapes in tomato sauce for my young son. His favourite character is Pikachu and he was particularly excited about having the meal and digging out his favourite Pokemon. Imagine his dismay when, despite Pikachu being the main character featured on the can, he discovered that there is no Pikachu spaghetti shape! I thought that maybe he wasn't looking at the pasta properly but upon checking the can, I can see that it mentions all the other characters that are included, but sadly no Pikachu. I now have to deal with an upset son and I wonder if there is anything you could do to ease his misery?

Yours sincerely,

A concerned parent"

Within a few days I'd received an apology letter from Heinz, and a voucher for £10. The Pokemon shapes had only cost me 5p originally; I'd bought them from the damaged cans section. What's more, they mentioned in their letter that they would get their designers to work on the problem and make sure that Pikachu was not used as the main character on the can any more, to avoid any other children being similarly disappointed. Six months later, while in the supermarket, I saw the new can: Pikachuless. The power of the pen!

More recently I wrote a similar letter to Mr. Cadbury about their chocolate-covered peanuts. Down at the bottom of the bag I found a solitary peanut that had somehow evaded its chocolatey fate. My letter described how I didn't like plain peanuts, I only like chocolate ones, so I couldn't eat the last peanut in the bag. I got a voucher for £5 for my troubles. The worst part of it is that my complaint was genuine. I really didn't like plain peanuts and I had to throw that one away. On the plus side I bought myself a nice big box of Milk Tray with the proceeds.

*　　　*　　　*　　　*　　　*

In the pub last night my drummer friend Sven turned to me, after telling me about how he was now quitting his day job to go out on the road, and asked if I'd be interested in joining him. Not full time, just standing in every now and again if their guitar player couldn't make it to gigs. Being in a touring covers band paid good money and given that it would only be once in a blue moon I said I'd think about it. This conversation followed:

Phone Monkey: Wait, what if I learn all the twenty-odd songs and put all that work in, then I'm only needed twice a year or something? That'd be a lot of work for not a lot of money.

Sven: You don't have to learn how to play the songs.

Phone Monkey: I don't understand. Of course I do.

Sven: No, just listen to them on the way to the gig and play it by ear.

Phone Monkey: I don't think you understand the concept of my rudimentary guitar playing. I can't improvise 24 songs that I barely know.

Sven: You don't have to be plugged in or anything.

Phone Monkey: Huh? (Puzzled look on my face)

Sven: No, in the olden days everyone had a backing track that just had backing vocals and keyboards and a click track on, and the band played along with that. Nowadays it's gone the opposite way and the backing track has everything on it apart from vocals. Basically the music will be coming out of the speakers, and only the drums and vocals are performed live. You just have to stand there and pretend you know how to play the songs.

Phone Monkey: So I'd be miming? For £100 a night?!

Sven: Yeah, it's dead easy. I mean, if you can play the songs then by all means plug in and play along if you want, but there's really no need to.

Phone Monkey: I can't believe what I'm hearing. This is bizarre!

Sven: So are you in?

Phone Monkey: Hell yes, I'm in!

The strange world of the touring musician... You didn't even have to be a musician any more!

*   *   *   *   *

Obviously having forgotten about the incident where he told Sarah off, Nizza went back to his old ways today, offering to make her a cup of tea. He'd become a figure of ridicule in our office, with how much of a dirty old perv he'd become. Sarah played on it, and it was fun to see him squirm when she flirted with him.

Over the weekend I went out for a drink with a couple of my fellow Phone Monkeys from this new job, and there was a young lad who worked here called Ryan, all fresh-faced and innocent. Upon reaching the height of drunkenness he proceeded to tell me that he'd been scared to talk to me all week because I came across as intimidating and inaccessible. I'm not really sure how he came to that conclusion since nobody else did.

This job was a constant learning curve and today I learnt something new, which didn't really please the customer. She'd had her gold necklace, valued at around £500, stolen from her whilst on holiday. She had a police report, witnesses, a receipt, and everything else she could possibly need to make a claim. I asked her how old the necklace was and she said six years. As we usually do, once I'd taken all the details of the claim I put her on hold while I checked the policy wording to see if there was any reason why we wouldn't cover this claim. I found, much to my amazement, that travel insurance didn't cover anything you were claiming for that was over five years old. We had to apply depreciation to any item, whether it was taking 10% off for a one-year-old item, or 90% off it was four years old. But I had to sit there and tell this woman that even though the value of the necklace would have gone up due to increasing gold prices, she wouldn't be able to get a penny for it by claiming with us. She shouted a bit. She demanded to speak to my team leader who she shouted at some more, then she hung up. My advice, kids: Make sure that anything you take on holiday with you is covered by your home insurance on a Personal Possessions policy to avoid this situation!

A new girl started today: Amanda. I'd only been here a week and I was already taking calls. She'd been working for this same company at the Sheffield site for over 6 months and she was AWFUL! She sounded really nervous on the phone. She sat next to our team leader who very much regretted sitting there, and leaned over to him every minute or so to tell him every detail of every call she took. Then she put people on hold to ask really obvious questions. Today I saw her hold up a letter in front of him, which clearly said: "iPhone 6, BARRED", and it had the letterhead of the company who'd issued the phone. Amanda asked if this letter had everything we needed to see on a document to prove that the phone had been barred. It would have been funny if it wasn't so annoying. I got the impression she'd been shipped over to our Manchester office because the people of Sheffield had exiled her.

Creative Monkey

Day Seven

Given that it was throwing it down this morning and my Batman brolly was sadly handleless, I considered taking one of my daughter's umbrellas: a bright yellow Pikachu umbrella with ears and a big smiley face on it. I eventually decided against this and figured I'd weather the storm. Upon stepping out of the house, I realised that this was no ordinary rainstorm. This was what I refer to as Big Fat Rain. The kind that makes you look like a drowned rat in less than a second. I stepped back into the house, desperate for other options to avoid the weather. My housemate handed me another umbrella: A beautiful pink one with bright love hearts all over it. I got halfway down the street and received more than a few funny looks, before turning around and going back home again to deposit my embarrassing umbrella. I walked to work unprotected, and sat in the office in a little puddle of water.

Little niggles could really become massive issues with me in the workplace, and the thing I'd found that annoyed me the most was when Phone Monkeys took the details of a claim over the phone, and didn't write many of those details down. I'd seen claims that just literally said "Car crash" or "Items stolen", which offered virtually no help when I was trying to decide if a crime or accident was avoidable and whether or not I wanted to pay out on a claim. If the offending people are reading this book now, please write fuller comments! I quite often had to ring the customers to get them to reiterate what had happened to cause them to claim. This got them very angry, having to go through it again, especially as it had been a month since they first filed the claim and obviously nothing had been done about it since that initial call.

I took a call from a woman today who'd crashed her car into somebody else's. Sadly she only had Third Party Fire and Theft cover, which meant that we would pay for the damage done to the other person's car, but that the woman who caused the accident wouldn't get anything to repair or replace her car which, in this instance, had to be written off. This didn't bother her. The car itself wasn't worth very much. What she was more bothered about was the fact that she had a large bag of... how do I put this politely? Hmm. It was sex toys. She had a big bag of them and as she'd crashed, her car had burst into flames and her extensive collection, valued at around £1000, had gone up with it. She was lucky to escape with her life by all accounts, but I had to inform her that we wouldn't cover her for any of the loss. She wasn't an Ann Summers representative based on her job title on the claim, and I didn't dare ask her why she was carrying around £1000 worth of sex toys. Be warned in case you carry a large collection of them round in your boot, sex toys probably won't be covered on your car insurance.

*   *   *   *   *

When I was growing up, my uncle Jack was known in the area as being a Del-Boy type of wheeler-dealer, and this influenced me to sell things at school myself. I did drawings of various comic book characters, I made little cardboard toys, I'd sell comics I'd bought at the car boot sale for twice their value and various other money-making schemes. This continued well into my twenties and eventually led to me setting up my own business selling comics, all based on ideas I'd gleaned from spending time with my uncle Jack. He didn't ever really make any money with his deals though, and I was always hearing stories of deals that had gone wrong. The best of those stories for me, and which summed up his life of buying and selling, was this: I was only young, maybe six or seven, and he came into the front room, all excited that he'd managed to pick up a brand new VCR (for those young people among you, that's a Video Cassette Recorder – this was the 1980s) and he'd only paid the minimal sum of £5 for it. He was ever so proud. He pulled out a shiny new video that he'd just bought from the local shop, which had probably cost more than the machine itself, and proceeded to try and put the video in the player. It wouldn't go in. He scratched his head and checked that he'd plugged it in properly. Yep, the lights were on, everything should be fine. Again he pushed the video into the slot but it just wouldn't go. Eventually he got frustrated with it and sat down with a screwdriver to take it apart. When he opened it up he found that it was completely full of toast. We have no idea where the toast came from or how long it had been in there, or even why anyone would put toast in a video player, but he never did manage to get that VCR working again.

*   *   *   *   *

I overheard new girl Amanda on a call to a customer today, where she told him that his claim would be dealt with within 2 days. The company line is that we have a 28-day turnaround and we were currently 8 days behind our schedule since it was summer and we were getting lots of travel claims in. We were going to be getting an angry call from that customer in three days time asking why her claim hadn't been sorted yet.

Day Eight

On the way to work this morning I heard loud, stampy footsteps behind me. I turned quickly, clammy with fear that the giant rabbit was back to drag me into its burrow but, even more disturbingly, there was no one there!

Training Day One

How bizarre, considering I'd been doing the job for nearly two weeks. They took me into a room and explained about fault and non-fault car accidents, cancellation and curtailment on travel claims, and that your wedding insurance wouldn't cover you if you just decided to break up with your fiancé(e). The training lasted approximately fifteen minutes. I didn't learn one thing I hadn't already picked up from working on the phones. Sigh.

A teammate's phone wasn't working today so while management ran around trying to find a new one for her, she plugged her headset into my phone and listened to the calls I was taking. She kept trying to distract me, hiding my pen, switching my computer monitor off when I was typing notes, and poking my arm. It was annoying, but we were having a laugh. Then at one point a customer whose claim I was settling asked if he could pop us on mute for a minute while he asked his wife something. I turned to my sidekick and said, "I've settled this claim and he's gonna get more money than he expected. He totally wants to make love to me."

This is the point at which I realised that it was he who had muted me, not the other way round and that not only would he have heard me say that, but also that the call was being recorded and my managers would have a record of it if he decided to put in a complaint. My stomach was in knots. When he came back on the phone he didn't mention it. I was hoping that the high settlement of his claim would be enough to keep him quiet!

Sarah went into the kitchen to make a cup of tea and Nizza was already in there. It was quite a tight squeeze in there so Nizza offered to make Sarah her tea and sent her back in the office. She'd apparently made some comment to him about how she only went to make a cup of tea so she could escape being on the phone for a little bit. He'd retorted with "You're such a naughty girl." Blurp. All of our mouths filled with vomit. He came back in with her cup of tea a few minutes later and we couldn't help but wonder if it contained Nizza's own "special milk".

In my old job the team leaders were constantly going on about how our "wrap" had to be kept to a minimum (15 seconds per call). Basically "wrap" was the time you used to type up your notes after a call had ended. Some calls didn't need any notes other than "Claim form sent", while some required full paragraphs writing about fraud concerns and extenuating circumstances which meant the customer had left it six months before making a claim. In this new job, the wrap was three minutes. And if we didn't finish the notes by the end of three minutes? Then we could go on "busy" for as long as it took to finish up what we were doing. I couldn't believe the relaxed attitude management had towards this in the new job. Maybe because I worked in claims now, and it was vital that I didn't miss anything out that was relevant to the case, but it essentially gave us carte blanche to avoid work, literally for as long as we wanted to. This came in very handy for people who came into work hungover. I'm not saying I was ever one of those people.

The first call I took this morning was for someone who called up and said her iTouch had been stolen while she was on holiday. I felt really old. I had to ask her what an iTouch was. She explained it to me and I'm still not really sure what it is or what it does.

Financial Crash

Day Nine

Nizza crossed the line today, and possibly landed himself in some very hot water. As his shift ended he sent an email to Sarah, which she quickly forwarded to the rest of us. It went like this:

"Hi Sarah,

I'm off next week but I'll still be up in Manchester, doing various things. I wondered if you'd like to go out for a meal with me on Wednesday night, all on me of course. I get lonely when I'm up in Manchester away from my friends and family and some company would be nice. I'd be happy to pay for your transport home afterwards as well.

Nigel"

We discussed this in some depth before our shifts finished, and we agreed that if one of us fellow Phone Monkeys had asked her out for a meal or for drinks it wouldn't have seemed weird at all. We talked to her on a daily basis and we were all becoming friends, despite not having known each other for very long. Nizza, on the other hand, rarely spoke to anyone, other than to discuss claims with them. Sarah was understandably freaked out and, although Nizza was a nice enough guy, this was one step too far and she had to report him to HR. What would come of that was anybody's guess, but every time he was anywhere near Sarah there was an uncomfortable atmosphere, and it would probably be in everyone's best interest if he were to leave, or at least be re-assigned to another office in the building.

Earlier in the day he'd dropped a pen on the floor by accident, and asked Sarah to bend down and get it for him, knowing full well that she was wearing a skirt and he'd get to see a flash of her bum. He sweated a lot too, even when it was cold, which made him even creepier. He was like a huge, evil slug.

One of the things I'd like to talk about, although I'm sure it's been mentioned before, was cold callers. I had the benefit in my job that I didn't call customers, unless I needed urgent information about the claim they'd filed. I would never be trying to sell anything to them and the only time I talked to a customer was if they called me to make a claim. There wasn't much that I hated more than sitting down to a nice dinner, then being rudely interrupted by a phone call which turned out to be someone trying to sell me some new windows, trying to get me to pay £2 a month into some weird cat charity, or convinced that their mobile phone upgrade package would be far superior to what I currently had.

My way of combating these evil fiends, especially since they were interfering with my "home time" was to come up with a variety of tricks, mostly learnt from my dad, to get rid of these people. My friends think I'm very odd when they see me do it. They say they're only doing their job and it's not their fault, but come on, they all used to work in call centres too, doing cold calling, so they're the enemy! My favourite of my dad's tricks was this: The phone would ring. They ask for Mr Phone Monkey. I would tell them that I'm not Mr Phone Monkey but I would go and get him. At this point I would put the phone down on the side and walk off... never to return. I liked to look at my phone an hour later to see how long the hapless Phone Monkey waited in silence before deciding to hang up on the call. If his job was anything like mine, he'd get in trouble for hanging up the call before the customer did. Hopefully they would then put a black mark next to my name on their list... and never call again.

Another one is what I called "The Deaf Man". They would call up, I would answer and they would tell me they want to sell me some new windows for my flat. I would say, "No thank you, I already have a cat." Then the consultant would have to explain that he said flat, not cat. Then I would tell him that I don't want to buy a flat either, I was happy where I was. At this point it would be difficult to hold back my giggles. If they got as far as trying to explain more slowly what they were selling, I would tell them that I didn't live in a flat at all, I lived in a tent in a park since my wife left me, so I had no windows to replace. They wouldn't know what to do with this information. Mission accomplished. Confused Phone Monkey would hang up.

My final trick is when you get a call from one of those automated phone services, usually asking if you've ever taken out a loan because you may be entitled to a PPI refund, and that the banks had set aside billions of pounds for it. As soon as the message starts, press 5. No matter what the company is, this will always take you out of their automated system and put you through to a Phone Monkey. Then when they answer, don't say anything. This might seem a bit petty but I figure that if they want to waste my time (I'd never taken out a loan or anything else that would have included PPI anyway), then I'd waste 30 seconds of one of their employees' time too. Eventually they would hang up. The best part of this one is, because I'd pressed 5, it registered on their system that I wanted to speak to them but that no further action was taken, and they would then call back at the same time the following day. Then you had the opportunity to go right ahead and try one of the other little pranks which you read about above. Double win. When you get bored of these tricks it's no trouble to save their number in your phone as Spam 1, Spam 2 etc., and then block incoming calls from those numbers.

I was glad that my new job put me in a positive mood for a change. It was not as strict, not as stressful, and everyone I worked with was nice. A lot of the work has the odd crazy rule to follow, and I still occasionally got shouted at by customers, but for now I was happy.

Day One Hundred and Sixty-Six

157 days have passed since my last entry in this... well I suppose you could call it a diary. Rather than bore you with details of everything you've missed, I'm going to break it down to the most important events for you. The most important by far is Nigel, or Nizza as he was known, and his swift exit from the company. After he sent the email to 23-year-old Sarah, inappropriately asking her to join him for a meal, she had to report him to our manager. It hadn't been an isolated incident; he'd been buying her chocolates and flirting very publicly with her, and it was becoming difficult for her to work with him. He was a big slimy frog, and more importantly he was twice her age.

As expected from a big company faced with a tricky situation like this, they chickened out of firing him, presumably to avoid him appealing against the charges made against him. What he'd been doing was sexual harassment, there was no doubt about that, but it could have dragged on for months and caused a lot of upset for young Sarah. So when the managers of the company took him into a room one morning, we presumed it would all be over and he'd be handed his P45. What they actually did was tell him that as he didn't actually work for our company and he was an outside contractor, they weren't going to renew his rolling monthly contract. He essentially had four weeks left to work there, which they agreed to let him take as paid leave. They never discussed his harassment of Sarah. They just said that they didn't have the resources to keep him on. That he was an unnecessary expense for the company.

For the rest of that day he was slagging off our company to us. He was very vociferous about how they'd "shafted" him. And when Sarah mentioned someone going on a tea run, Nizza very sleazily told her "I want one from you by the end of the day." He didn't even make any attempt to hide his innuendo as he flashed her a dirty old man smile.

As the end of the day arrived, Sarah was getting nervous that he might say something to her in one last attempt to win her heart on his last day at the company. True enough, he started walking towards her, shaking two other members of staff's hands on the way, before slimily approaching her. For a second it was very awkward. Everyone in the office knew what a slimeball he was, and that he'd been trying to get into Sarah's pants, and we all watched with baited breath. There was a deafening silence in the room and as he got to her, he didn't try to shake her hand, he just stood unnervingly close to her, pointed his finger at her, and said, "Don't be naughty, you."

Then he turned and walked out of the door, and we never saw him again.

In the weeks that followed, we discovered the legacy of his work with us. Virtually every claim we looked into had been reviewed at some point by Nizza... incorrectly. Every single piece of work he'd touched had to be re-assessed, meaning that the money spent on hiring him as an outside consultant had been completely wasted because now we were all spending inordinate amounts of hours undoing all his mistakes. Overtime had to be introduced so we could sort this unholy mess out.

On a drunken night out with Sarah and some of my friends from my band, I accidentally told her about my Phone Monkey books. This was dangerous because I knew she could be a bit of a loudmouth sometimes, and I was suddenly very concerned that my secret might come out, and I might have to make a sharp exit from yet another job, for dissing them in the pages of my books. What actually happened was that she was very good at keeping my secret, and was rather impressed that she was a character in a book. She phoned her mum and dad and they downloaded copies of it so they could read about what their daughter got up to at work.

What she didn't like, however, was my interpretation of her. She didn't think she was rude to customers, and felt that I misrepresented her booming voice. I stand by my description of her though. What she did surprised me though. She went home the night after reading the book with her in it, and started working on her own Phone Monkey book, a rebuttal of my character description, and some details of funny claims she'd dealt with. I joked that she could name it Ms Phone Monkey, to mimic the Pac-Man sequel. I don't know if she'll ever finish it; she's not as committed or obsessed with writing as me, but it was strange reading the work she'd done on it so far, knowing that I could be influencing a spin-off book!

She also told me on a drunken night out that she intended to write a weekly fashion blog, and try to get a women's magazine to publish it. She asked me if I'd do the illustrations for her and I agreed. Then the following day at work I brought it up, asking if she'd written any of the blog so I could get to work on my first drawing for it. She stared blankly at me. She had no idea what I was talking about. We'd discussed it at length the night before and now she had forgotten all about it, and even said that it didn't sound like something she'd be interested in doing. How bizarre.

One of the parts of my job that cause the most upset, both for staff and customers, was when a family member had died and we had to ask for a death certificate. To make matters worse, we needed them to send us the original document, not a copy, so we could check that it was genuine. The number of times I'd been shouted at was ridiculous, and I'd even had people tell me that they didn't want to make the claim because the death was too fresh in their mind and they'd rather not think about it, sometimes abandoning a claim for which they could have been paid thousands of pounds.

Bad Day

Day One Hundred and Sixty-Seven

Sarah took a call today, from some holidaymakers who had a large quantity of Euros which they didn't want to carry around with them. Even though there had been a safe which they could have paid a small amount to use, they had instead opted to put the money "somewhere safe"… although I think their idea of what was safe, and everyone else's idea were two very different things. They put the money, about 600 Euros, in the microwave. I kid you not. Then they went out for the day, had a lovely day at the beach, and came back to the room that evening, to cook themselves some supper. They put some food in the oven and decided they wanted some peas to go with their meal. Rather than boil them on the hob, they decided to put them in a bowl in the microwave.

Euros, like most money, had a foil strip interweaved into them. It was to stop people easily counterfeiting money. It was also very handy for starting fires in microwaves, it seemed. Within seconds of the peas starting to cook, the money had burst into flames and they stopped the microwave straight away, throwing water on the money in an attempt to save it. Sadly, it was too late. All of the money was at least partially destroyed, meaning that no one, not even the bank, would accept it. How had they not noticed that there was something in the microwave when they put the bowl of peas in it? The person who called to make the claim also had the audacity to claim that she was a chef by trade, although I'm not sure how she felt that made her look anything other than more stupid.

So when they phoned us up and spoke to Sarah about it, she had to tell them that the money was not covered on their insurance policy. Had the money been in the safe when it set on fire then it would have been covered. But because they stupidly set fire to their own money in the microwave, they were not covered. They weren't happy, and even went as far as sending in the burnt money, which was the source of much hilarity in the office. If there'd been an Idiot Clause in their policy then they might have been covered.

While my Phone Monkey books were achieving some success on the Amazon chart, the same couldn't be said for one of my other offerings. I wrote a kids' book under my real name, not anonymously like this book was. Basically it was a picture book. A mixture of photos and some sketches. It was a cross between a kids' book and a very basic comic strip. The only problem with it was that I'd only sold one copy of it in the nine months it had been on sale. It recieved a five-star review on Amazon, which I'd hoped would boost sales (and surprisingly I didn't write the review myself), but sadly it looked like it was literally going to be the worst selling book on Amazon. EVER. My mum and a few other people told me it had been recommended to them in an email about kids' books. I still didn't sell any more copies off the back of that advertising. I'd print its name here so you could go and discover it... but I get the feeling you wouldn't buy it either.

I learnt another interesting fact today: There have been more insurance claims (obviously mostly fraudulent) made for lost Rolex watches than there have been Rolex watches made.

Day One Hundred and Sixty-Eight

Amanda took a call from a customer today who was being irrational and shouting at her. As the call ended and the customer hung up, she said out loud, "Did you hear him shouting? What a f****** a***hole," before realizing that he hadn't actually hung up yet, and not only would her not-so-polite comment have been recorded on our internal phone system, but he actually heard her say it. Then she spent five minutes, nervously apologizing to him as he shouted at her some more, telling her how he was going to get her sacked.

There was another need for an Idiot Clause in policies today. A man rang up and told me that his brother had phoned and said that their dad had died and he had to journey home for the funeral. So he'd cancelled his family holiday, gone back up north with his wife and three kids, where they'd gone straight to his brother's house to find out the details of what would be happening at the funeral the following day. Upon reaching the house, he was told that his brother had been very drunk on the night that the phone call had taken place. He had no recollection of telling his brother on the phone that their dad had died... and in fact, he hadn't. He was still very much alive; in fact he was sat right there in his brother's kitchen. With the travel company refusing to reinstate his booking, he'd decided to give me a ring to see what he could claim for. The simple answer: Nothing. Sigh.

Amanda continued with her inappropriate comments at lunchtime today, as she informed all the men of the group that if they ever bought chocolates for their girlfriends, what they were essentially doing was buying themselves a fat girlfriend.

A Bad Egg

Day One Hundred and Sixty-Nine

When a customer made a claim related to a medical condition, we had to investigate the condition online to see if anything they had previously seen their doctor for had any relevance to their current illness. Basically if they had symptoms of the illness before they bought their travel insurance then they could not claim on their policy. The number of times I'd had to look at pages of breast examinations and weird penis diseases must make our IT Department think I'm trawling for porn at work. One customer, had a cyst at the base of his spine. It burst, literally ripping him a new a***hole in the bottom of his back, which then proceeded to leak excrement. Blurp. Hope you're not eating your dinner as you read this!

The team leaders had become so obsessed with us not wasting time that whenever we printed anything off, we weren't allowed to go and get our printing ourselves. Because the printer was in another office which was linked to ours, we had a printing monitor person, who had to go and collect all the printing at the end of each day. Yesterday I accidentally printed a claim form out twice, and the nominated printing monitor was Amanda. Basically, everyone else had real work to do and our team leaders were so concerned about the abysmal quality of her work that they were desperate to find anything for her to do that she couldn't make a total mess of. She approached me yesterday afternoon and wagged her finger at me. "You're very naughty," she scolded me. "You've printed this twice." I got the feeling she was flirting with me, which I found a little creepy.

Then when she went home we all sat round and discussed how it would be funny, just for one day, for all of us to print two copies of every single document we printed. Most things we printed were getting sent out directly to the customers. So today we did just that, but the plan kind of fell apart when Amanda didn't say anything to anybody and just sent all the documents out. Every customer would be sent two separate letters about whatever we were writing to them about. Can you imagine opening up a letter that says, "Sorry, your claim has been declined," then opening the next letter and seeing exactly the same message? We couldn't believe she could have missed the double-printing on the 50 or so letters that were sent out so we've decided we're going to continue doing it every day until she realises.

A customer called Mr Robinson called today, as he has every day for the last two weeks. He'd claimed that his suitcase had been damaged by the airline when he went to Spain last month, and he'd sent us in a huge pile of receipts and a long list of items which belonged to him. Because of the huge amount of things he was claiming for, the claim was taking a lot longer than usual to process, and he knew just how to wind us up. Despite the office closing at 5.30pm, he would always ring at 5.29 and ask to speak to a manager. The managers always left at 5. He'd been made aware of this a number of times but still he kept ringing back, shouting abuse at whoever he got on the phone with, because his claim still hadn't been paid out.

I looked into the notes of his claim and could see that he'd shouted at every single member of the team at some point, but I could see that most of the claim had been analysed and we would probably be able to make a payment the next day. I told him this, and he asked how much he'd be getting. I told him that there would be three separate excesses for him to pay, as the claim was for items belonging to him, his wife and his daughter. This only enraged him further, and he tried to claim that all the items he was claiming for were his. I pointed out that there were children's t-shirts and women's dresses. He paused for a moment before confirming that all those clothes did indeed belong to him. Now if we ever believe that a customer has lied to us about any aspect of a claim we have to report them to the fraud department. Because I couldn't picture him wearing children's and ladies' dresses, I had to send his claim to be double-checked by the fraud team. I didn't tell Mr. Robinson this of course, because I would never have got home. And I especially didn't want to tell him that there was a 4-week backlog of fraud claims. I hoped not to be there the next time he phoned.

Pre-Existing Idiot

214

Day One Hundred and Seventy

Amanda's onslaught of flirting continued today as she kept asking me about my weekend, and what I liked to do for fun. Before today I'd never had an actual conversation with her about anything. I found her weird and awkward, which was no bad thing in itself necessarily, but I really wasn't looking for a girlfriend. And relationships that began in the workplace would be a definite no-no for me.

She'd also started to become a clone of Sarah from our team too. She was always asking her where she got her clothes from, then turned up to work wearing the exact same outfits, with her hair combed in the same style as Sarah's, even going as far as cutting her long hair short in order to be a more perfect clone.

*   *   *   *   *

Three years ago I was living on what I referred to affectionately as Crime Alley. It was a small street with a train which ran past the end of it. The strange thing about Crime Alley was that one side of the street was Crime Alley and the other side of the street was Crime Avenue. Two streets in one. So there were two number fourteens on the same street, which made it a nightmare for the postman, who I think struggled to even read, let alone post things to the correct house. At least three times a week, my neighbours at the opposite number fourteen would have to come and post things through my door which had been mistakenly put through their letterbox, and I would always return the favour with their post. One day, because it was hot and summery, I decided to leave my front door open to get some fresh air through the house. The postman came to the door and handed me my post. Well, not my post. 14 Crime Avenue's post. Then he told me how he'd had a pile of letters which needed to be signed for, for various people in my area, and that he'd gone for his dinner one day and sat in his car in a supermarket's car park. He'd read a newspaper and thrown it on the seat beside him when he was done. Then he drove over to the huge recycle bin and threw the paper in. It wasn't until he drove away that he realised the Recorded Delivery letters had somehow become tucked into the newspaper and were now on their way to the recycling plant. So the next time something you send gets lost in the post, think of my old postman and assume that there are probably similarly special people working up and down the country.

My street seemed to have nothing but criminals on it. I saw loads of drug deals take place, and one of my neighbours had seen all the bookcases of comics in my front room and decided to pop round and see me. He said he also collected comics and showed me a tattoo on his arm of a character called Pitt. I then sold him some of my Pitt comics, and also offered him a beer. I asked him why he was always at home. He told me that he used to be "an enforcer" for a local gang but when he got really badly stabbed one day, he decided he'd had enough and was now living on state benefits which recognized him as being legally disabled. I told him that he seemed fine to me, and he then proceeded to lift up his t-shirt and show me a scar that ran from his navel to his collarbone. He hadn't just been stabbed, he'd been cut open, and most of his internal organs had been damaged, making it impossible to do anything physical for long periods of time without being in agony. The good thing about living on Crime Alley, I decided, was that because all the criminals lived there, there was never any trouble and I always felt completely safe. You wouldn't take a dump in your own kitchen, so to speak.

*   *   *   *   *

Sarah's call of the day was from a man who had cancelled the holiday he and his girlfriend had intended to take, because she'd left him. The problem had been that he'd developed a sexually transmitted disease, and as she didn't have it, she surmised he must have cheated on her. So she'd packed her bags and left, leaving him to cancel this holiday. Sarah had to tell him that he couldn't claim anything on his insurance because basically all he'd done was just decide to not go on holiday. The illness hadn't prevented him going. He'd just chosen not to go.

216

The story had an upside though, despite him losing all the money he'd paid out for his trip. He said that after extensive tests, doctors had discovered that the infection he had couldn't have been sexually transmitted, and he'd actually had it since birth, although it had been dormant until very recently. He'd told his ex-girlfriend this and she'd welcomed him back with open arms. So the story had a happy ending, after all. They still couldn't go on the holiday though, because he'd cancelled it.

Can You Hear Me?

Day One Hundred and Seventy-One

When the manager came into the office, it was usually a sign that one of us had done something wrong. When she came in today and asked to speak to me and Amanda at the same time, I had no idea what to expect.

Manager: Phone Monkey, I know you were doing really well in the job and that you'd been thinking of training to be a specialist or team leader but I've just had some bad news. This is for you too, Amanda.

Phone Money: Sounds ominous.

Manager: Three of our largest insurers, clients who your team handle the claims for, have decided to move to a different claims handling company. This wouldn't be a problem if they were some of our smaller clients but these are our three biggest clients, and we're going to be losing a lot of business. The workload of the team is going to be pretty much halved.

Amanda: So what does this mean for me and Phone Monkey? Why are we in here?

Manager: Well unfortunately we have to let the two most recent members of staff go, which is you and Phone Monkey. We can let you work until the end of the month but we can't keep you on past that. I know it's December and this couldn't have come at a worse time with Christmas and New Year and all that, but there really isn't anything I can do about it. There just isn't enough work for us to keep you on.

Phone Monkey: Oh.

Manager: If there are any jobs within the company that come available then by all means, let me know and I'll get you a guaranteed interview. We'd rather keep you on than send you out there with no job at this time of year

There were a couple of posts available so I'd been given time off the phone to update my CV. Amanda was applying for the same role as me, and actually asked me for tips on what to write on her application, even though she was my competition!

Acapella

Day One Hundred and Seventy-Five

Amanda decided not to apply for the internal job but instead had a job interview this morning to be a receptionist for a health clinic. I can't imagine what their customers would think if Amanda was their first point of contact, with her nervousness and general ability to make a hash out of everything she did. Her new job would be on the same pay as here, but pro-rata just for three days a week. She thought that meant she'd do three days' work but get paid for the full week. We tried explaining pro-rata to her but she looked confused and when she got the job we didn't have the heart to tell her that it would be a six grand pay cut in reality. She'd find out the hard way, we supposed.

As the day drew to a close, the people from the office next door, the place we called The Scary Room because of the way everyone turned and stared at you when you walked in the room, came in to get me. They took my computer. They took my notebooks. They took my little blue plastic pen holder. They were desperate for a new member of staff so I'd been told that I didn't have to finish my month as a Phone Monkey. They wanted me to start on Monday instead. I sat at an empty desk for the last half hour of my shift, wondering if I'd made the right decision. I was never going to speak to a customer ever again.

DATA MANAGEMENT MONKEY

I had a bit of a plan. When the opportunity to move to a different department came up, I thought a new job would be rife with new opportunities to discover more insanity in another area of the insurance business. I thought I'd start my first day and learn about a million and one things that I could tell you. So what did the new job entail? I did not have the first clue. Hadn't the foggiest. My new role was one of bewilderment and confusion. I didn't know if I was doing my job right or not, I had no actual training, and I didn't even know what kind of products my department dealt with, or sold, or insured or anything. Sigh.

They showed me how to do lots of really complicated processes and I nodded and smiled like I understood what was happening but inside I was screaming because I wasn't very good with computers and I didn't really have a clue what was going on. I was beginning to think that misleading them into thinking I was good with Excel had been a mistake.

So this is it for Phone Monkey.

I hope you've enjoyed my adventures, and just remember: The next time you speak to a Phone Monkey, you have to remember that the automaton you're speaking to is a person too. A person who probably has more important things on their mind than how to help you solve your problem.

EPILOGUE

I hadn't planned to write an epilogue. I hate it when a story finishes and then some ego-filled author decides to go and ruin it all by adding some extra information that spoils everything that went before. I hope this isn't one of those times. When I came to put this book together, I had three previous Phone Monkey books to work with, which had all been previously available to digitally download. I took them off the website whose name I'm not allowed to mention here, but which shares the name as that rainforest in South America, compiled them into this one volume, and wrote what was essentially Phone Monkey Volume 4 for inclusion in this book, to add a suitable ending to my trials and tribulations as a Phone Monkey. As I was putting the last few comic strips together I thought I'd check on Amazon that the original Phone Monkey books had been deleted properly, and I searched "Phone Monkey Anonymous" (the original books being written anonymously like this one). Much to my surprise, the book below popped up:

I had no idea what it was but luckily it allowed me to search the index of the book, where I found references to "Phone Monkey : The Secret Diary of a Frustrated Call Centre Worker" on two pages. I was intrigued. Why was my story being mentioned in this book?

In a bizarre case of life imitating art imitating life, someone (Ronald H Humphrey to be more precise) had written a book about leadership theories in business, and had referenced my book in a section called "Phone Monkey Or Agent With A Mission?"

For somebody unknown like me, this was very cool. When I first put pen to paper on this blog/series of short books/fully-finished book, I never dreamed that a professor at Virginia Commonwealth University in the United States would be analysing my book to see how it related to the world of business.

I emailed the author, told him my real name and address, and he sent me a copy of the book, which now takes pride of place on my bookshelf next to where I work, and which gets pulled out every time a new friend stops by to see me. They probably couldn't care less, but I'm really proud of it.

I think that brings the story full circle. Job done. I mean, I'd love to see a Phone Monkey TV series one day (which I may have already started writing...) but hey, one step at a time. Thanks for joining me on this wild ride. Phone Monkeys of the world... unite!

About The Author

After spending his teenage years drawing little comics that virtually no one read, our anonymous author went on to earn a degree in Animation at some Northern University. Then there was what we call "The Wilderness Years" where nothing seemed to happen for a bit, and then all of a sudden, at 29 years old, he decided to try his hand at writing, which over the years morphed into the book you now hold in your hands. The days of slaving away in call centres are long behind him now and he now runs his own business... although we can't tell you what he does because you'd be able to track him down and this book wouldn't be so anonymous then, would it?

If you have any comments or questions about Phone Monkey, please feel free to email him. He tries to reply to every email he gets but please remember that he's very busy and also very lazy, so it might take him a while to get back to you!

phonemonkeybooks@hotmail.com

19601117R00127

Printed in Great Britain
by Amazon